Wales Theatre Handbook

LLAWLYFR Y THEATR YNG NGHYMRU

A guide to professional drama and dance in Wales
Arweiniad i fyd drama a dawns proffesiynol yng Nghymru

Canolfan y Celfyddydau
Aberystwyth
Arts Centre

Aberystwyth Arts Centre, University of Wales, Aberystwyth SY23 3DE
Canolfan y Celfyddydau Aberystwyth, Prifysgol Cymru, Aberystwyth SY23 3DE

Tel/Ffôn +44 (0) 1970 622882 Fax/Ffacs+44 (0) 1970 622883

Wales Theatre Handbook Llawlyfr y Theatr yng Nghymru

First published in 2002 by: Aberystwyth Arts Centre, University of Wales, Penglais, Aberystwyth, Ceredigion, Wales SY23 3DE
Cyhoeddwyd gyntaf yn 2002 gan: Canolfan y Celfyddydau Aberystwyth, Prifysgol Cymru, Penglais, Aberystwyth, Ceredigion, Cymru SY23 3DE
Tel/Ffôn: 01970 622882 Fax/Ffacs: 01970 622883 Email/Ebost: lla@aber.ac.uk Web/Wê: www.aber.ac.uk/artscentre
Grant aided by: INTERREG II: PACT @ Temple Bar and Aberystwyth Arts Centre, Wales Arts International

THIS PROJECT IS PART-FUNDED BY WALES IRELAND INTERREG PROGRAMME
CAFODD Y PROSIECT HWN EI ARIANNU YN RHANNOL GAN RAGLEN INTERREG CYMRU IWERDDON

ISBN 1 872609 90 2

Acknowledgements / *Ein diolch i:*
Ginny Brink, Voluntary Arts Network; Yvonne O'Donovan, Creu Cymru - Wales Touring Agency;
Alan Hewson, Canolfan y Celfyddydau Aberystwyth Arts Centre; Cathy Hughes; Damian Randle; Howard Wright

Design/*Dylunio*: www.fbagroup.co.uk

Stones
Directed/Cyfarwyddwyd gan: Jill Greenhalgh
Photograph/Llun: Keith Morris

Contents

CYNNWYS

Introduction

The publication of the first Wales Theatre Handbook marks a significant milestone in the history of professional theatre and dance in Wales. The volume will serve as a resource to promote the performing arts from and within Wales both at home and internationally. In the context of devolution the role of the cultural industries of Wales in enhancing the identity, confidence and economic prosperity of the nation is gaining increased recognition; the wide range of creative expression which belongs to our theatre and dance companies and practitioners is poised to play a central part in this process of achieving a wider recognition for Wales in the world.

The development of professional theatre in both the languages of Wales has been rapid since its comparatively recent beginnings; its audience is sophisticated, having had access to work influenced by the involvement of Welsh practitioners with theatre from Scandinavia, Eastern Europe and the Mediterranean as well as elements of the Welsh literary tradition. Theatre and dance continues to be enriched by the presence of both languages and by the unique culture which they embrace. The network of professionally equipped arts venues provides a launching pad for the work and provides the opportunity for audiences also to experience a range of incoming performances from abroad.

The Handbook supplies for the first time a comprehensive directory of information for venues, companies, practitioners and promoters from Wales and the world who are interested in the creation, development and staging of theatre and dance from Wales.

The resources section aims to assist professionals and aspiring practitioners to access knowledge and skills necessary for progression in the industry.

In compiling the handbook, we have been impressed by the growing number of professionally equipped arts venues - this together with the new initiative of Creu Cymru, the Wales touring agency, providing a marker for progress in presenting the arts. To match this success in terms of production - new writing, new dance and theatre production - a period of sustained strategic support is needed. Financial and developmental provision for both presenters and producers of work must be realistic and informed by a knowledge of and respect for the work itself. In the wake of the National Assembly's new cultural strategy and the re-organisation of the Arts Council of Wales, we look forward to a period of creativity and consolidation in the performing arts.

Gill Ogden, Performing Arts Officer, Aberystwyth Arts Centre

Editors' Note

The publication is an initiative of Aberystwyth Arts Centre, with the financial support of Wales Arts International who will distribute the handbook to British Council offices around the world. Research for the project was also partially funded by the Interreg II programme as part of the PACT scheme to promote touring and co-operation between theatre companies and venues in Wales and Ireland. This publication is sister to the Irish Theatre handbook which served as an inspiration and example of good practice.

The existence of a thriving theatre and dance scene is inevitably delineated to a large extent by access to funding and other forms of support. However, in editing the listings for companies and individuals we have adopted a number of specific criteria not necessarily linked to the receipt of Arts Council of Wales support:

- A company is primarily defined as a group which has performed in a professional venue (or site-specific on a professional basis) during the last 3 years
- A venue is primarily defined as a building which regularly presents professional dance and theatre performances: a number of venues are included which occasionally present professional work to provide a more comprehensive view
- Similarly, listed festivals are those which actively programme a significant quantity of professional theatre and/or dance
- A practitioner is defined as an individual living and working mainly in Wales who provides expertise on a professional basis
- Listings in the playlist include new plays, devised works and choreographed pieces created and staged professionally within Wales by Wales-based practitioners within the last 10 years (1991-2001)

In some instances information about practitioners and organisations has been reluctantly omitted due to an insufficiency of available evidence. Whilst every care has been taken in researching and obtaining information for inclusion in the handbook, Aberystwyth Arts Centre cannot and does not endorse the standard of service provided by the individuals or companies listed.

Wales Theatre Website

A companion website, **www.theatre-wales.co.uk** will be re-launched 6 weeks after publication and will include all the information included in the handbook together with additional detail and supplementary descriptions of the works included in the playlist.

It is intended that both the website and the handbook will be updated in future years; the editor welcomes proposals for entry in future editions.

Gill Ogden, Keith Morris Editors
Dorry Spikes, Stuart Jones Assistant Editors

Cyflwyniad

Mae cyhoeddi Llawlyfr y Theatr yng Nghymru am y tro cyntaf yn garreg filltir bwysig yn hanes y byd theatr a dawns proffesiynol yng Nghymru. Bydd y gyfrol yn fodd i hyrwyddo celfyddydau perfformio Cymru gartref ac yn rhyngwladol. Yng nghyd-destun datganoli, mae cydnabyddiaeth gynyddol yn cael ei rhoi i rôl diwydiannau diwylliannol Cymru mewn gwella hunaniaeth, hyder a ffyniant economaidd a genedl; mae'r amrediad eang o weithgareddau creadigol ein cwmnïau ac ymarferwyr theatr a dawns yn barod i chwarae rhan ganolog yn y broses hon o gael cydnabyddiaeth ehangach i Gymru yn y byd hwn.

Mae datblygu theatr broffesiynol yn nwy iaith Cymru wedi digwydd yn gyflym ers y dechreuad yn gymharol ddiweddar; mae'r gynulleidfa yn soffistigedig, ac mae wedi gallu profi gwaith wedi'i ddylanwadu gan gysylltiadau ymarferwyr Cymru â'r theatr yn Sgandinafia, Dwyrain Ewrop a Môr y Canoldir yn ogystal ag elfennau o'r traddodiad llenyddol yng Nghymru. Mae byd y theatr a'r ddawns yn dal i gael ei gyfoethogi gan y ddwy iaith a'r diwylliant unigryw sy'n deillio ohonynt. Mae'r rhwydwaith o ganolfannau'r celfyddydau â chyfleusterau proffesiynol yn hybu'r gwaith ac yn rhoi cyfle hefyd i gynulleidfaoedd brofi amrywiaeth o berfformiadau o dramor.

Mae'r Llawlyfr yn cynnig, am y tro cyntaf, wybodaeth gynhwysfawr am ganolfannau, cwmnïau, ymarferwyr a hyrwyddwyr o Gymru a'r byd sydd â diddordeb mewn creu, datblygu a llwyfannu theatr a dawns o Gymru.

Mae'r adran adnoddau'n cynnig cymorth i bobl broffesiynol a phobl sy'n gobeithio mentro i'r diwydiant hwn ynghylch sut i ddod o hyd i'r wybodaeth a'r sgiliau sy'n rhaid eu cael er mwyn llwyddo.

Wrth i ni lunio'r llawlyfr, gwnaed argraff dda arnom gan y nifer gynyddol o ganolfannau'r celfyddydau â chyfleusterau modern a'r fenter newydd, Creu, yr asiantaeth deithio i Gymru. Mae'r rhain yn arwyddion o'r cynnydd sy'n cael ei wneud o ran cyflwyno'r celfyddydau. I gyd-fynd â'r llwyddiant hwn o ran cynhyrchu - ysgrifennu newydd, cynhyrchiadau dawns a theatr newydd - mae angen cyfnod o gefnogaeth strategol barhaus. Rhaid i gyflwynwyr a chynhyrchwyr gweithiau gael cymorth ariannol a chymorth i ddatblygu sy'n realistig, gan wybod fod eu gwaith yn cael ei ddeall a'i barchu. Yn dilyn strategaeth ddiwylliannol newydd y Cynulliad Cenedlaethol ac ad-drefnu Cyngor Celfyddydau Cymru, edrychwn ymlaen at gyfnod o greadigedd a chyfnerthiad yn y celfyddydau perfformio.

Gill Ogden, Swyddog Celfyddydau Perfformio, Canolfan y Celfyddydau Aberystwyth

Gair gan y Golygyddion

Mae'r cyhoeddiad yn fenter gan Ganolfan y Celfyddydau Aberystwyth gyda chymorth ariannol Celfyddydau Cymru Rhyngwladol, a fydd yn dosbarthu'r llawlyfr i swyddfeydd y Cyngor Prydeinig ledled y byd. Cafodd yr ymchwil ar gyfer y prosiect ei hariannu yn rhannol gan raglen Interreg II fel rhan o'r cynllun PACT i hyrwyddo teithio a chydweithredu rhwng cwmnïau a chanolfannau theatr yng Nghymru ac Iwerddon. Mae'r cyhoeddiad hwn yn cyd-fynd â Llawlyfr y Theatr yn Iwerddon, a fu'n ysbrydoliaeth ac yn enghraifft o arferion da.

Mae cael ffyniant ym myd y theatr a'r ddawns yn gorfod dibynnu i raddau helaeth ar y cymorth ariannol a chymorth arall y gellir cael hyd iddynt. Fodd bynnag, wrth olygu'r manylion am gwmnïau ac unigolion rydym wedi defnyddio nifer o feini prawf penodol nad ydynt o angenrheidrwydd yn gysylltiedig â chael cymorth gan Gyngor Celfyddydau Cymru.

- Diffinnir cwmni fel grŵp sydd wedi perfformio mewn canolfan broffesiynol (neu sydd wedi bod yn gysylltiedig â safle penodol ar sail broffesiynol) yn ystod y tair blynedd diwethaf

- Diffinnir canolfan yn anad dim fel adeilad sy'n cyflwyno perfformiadau theatr a dawns proffesiynol (er mwyn rhoi darlun mwy cynhwysfawr, cafodd nifer o ganolfannau sy'n cyflwyno gwaith proffesiynol yn achlysurol eu cynnwys)

- yn yr un modd, y gwyliau a restrir yw'r rhai sy'n cynnwys nifer sylweddol o berfformiadau theatr a/ neu ddawns proffesiynol yn eu rhaglenni

- Diffinnir ymarferwr fel unigolyn sy'n byw ac yn gweithio yn bennaf yng Nghymru ac sy'n cynnig arbenigedd yn broffesiynol

- Mae rhestr y perfformiadau yn cynnwys perfformiadau newydd o ddramâu, gweithiau dyfeisiedig a darnau wedi'u coreograffu a gafodd eu creu a'u llwyfannu yn broffesiynol yng Nghymru gan ymarferwyr sydd wedi'u lleoli yng Nghymru yn ystod y deng mlynedd diwethaf (1991-2001)

Mewn rhai achosion, o'n hanfodd, bu'n rhaid diystyru gwybodaeth am ymarferwyr a sefydliadau oherwydd diffyg tystiolaeth ddigonol. Er gwaethaf gofal mawr wrth ymchwilio a chael hyd i wybodaeth i'w chynnwys yn y llawlyfr, ni all, ac nid yw, Canolfan y Celfyddydau Aberystwyth yn cymeradwyo safon y gwasanaeth sy'n cael ei ddarparu gan yr unigolion neu'r cwmnïau a restrir.

Gwefan y Theatr yng Nghymru

Caiff gwefan gymar www.theatre-wales.co.uk ei hail-lansio chwe wythnos ar ôl cyhoeddi'r llawlyfr, a bydd yn cynnwys yr holl wybodaeth yn y llawlyfr ynghyd â manylion ychwanegol a disgrifiadau atodol o'r gweithiau yn rhestr y perfformiadau.

Y bwriad yw diweddaru'r wefan a'r llawlyfr yn y dyfodol; mae croeso i awgrymiadau ar gyfer pethau i'w cynnwys.

Gill Ogden, Keith Morris Golygyddion
Dorry Spikes, Stuart Jones Golygyddion Cynorthwyol

Wales Arts International is pleased to support the
Mae'n bleser gan Gelfyddydau Cymru Rhyngwladol gefnogi

Wales Theatre Handbook
Llawlyfr y Theatr yng Nghymru

We believe the publication will be invaluable to a whole range of people and organisations. It will help raise the profile of the rich and varied product that is available in Wales as well as provide a practical guide to promoters both domestic and international. We hope that readers of this handbook will take advantage of the talent available from Wales and learn to recognise the importance of Welsh theatre both in the UK and internationally.

Credwn y bydd y cyhoeddiad o werth amhrisiadwy i amrediad eang o bobl a sefydliadau. Bydd yn gymorth i godi proffil y cynnyrch cyfoethog ac amrywiol sydd ar gael yng Nghymru, yn ogystal â darparu arweiniad ymarferol i hyrwyddwyr yng Nghymru ac yn rhyngwladol. Gobeithiwn y bydd darllenwyr y llawlyfr hwn yn manteisio ar y doniau sydd ar gael yng Nghymru ac yn dysgu sut i adnabod pwysigrwydd y theatr Gymreig yn y DG a thramor.

Rosemary Edwards
International Arts Manager / *Rheolwraig Celfyddydua Rhyngwladol*

Companies

CWMNÏAU

Alma Theatre

Chapter Arts Centre, Market Rd, Canton
Cardiff CF5 1QE

Tel/Ffôn   **+44 (0) 29 2040 5949**
Email/Ebost **rabab.alma@talk21.com**

Artistic Director/Cyfarwyddwyr Artistig: **Rabab Ghazoul**

Artistic Policy Polisi Artistig:

Alma Theatre make work for space, bodies, they put text into space, around body, they make site specific work, solos, touring pieces. Narrative, its manufacture and distortion, and identity, its construction, demolition, feeds content as well as process. Audience, what it means, its relation to performance, and the individual's location of self within political and cultural landscapes informs their work. As does image, sound, silence, and the intersections between all of the above.

Company History Hanes y Cwmni:

Formed in 1993 in Cardiff, Alma Theatre premiered its first work in 1994, exploring language and body through the texts of Gertrude Stein. The company went on to tour productions (The Dress, How Soon Is Now) and create a series of site-specific works between 1996 and 1999 in locations to include a waterfront setting, back yard, stately home, castle grounds and disused warehouse. 1997 saw the creation of a festival of Wales wide contemporary performance, PLAYSTATION, and a solo site-specific work, The Arab Room, premiered in 1998, with showings at home and abroad. The company have presented work at international festivals, and experimental platforms in Wales, England and Europe. Collaboration has been an ongoing feature of the company's work, to include projects with international practitioners from Serbia, New Zealand, Norway, Ireland and Wales.

Past Productions Cynhyrchiadau'r Gorffennol:

The Belly; Belly II; The Dress; You Are Here (project of five separate site-specific performances over 2 year period); **How Soon Is Now; The Arab Room.**

Future Plans Cynlluniau at y dyfodol:

The premiere of **The Naming of the Storm** in April 2002, will follow with a tour of the piece throughout 2002/03. During this time, a series of site-specific collaborative works **Systematic**, with performance artists from Serbia, England and Canada will be in development for showings in 2003. 2004 sees the premiere of the company's next touring performance **Sly Shimmer**.

Cwmni Theatr Arad Goch

Stryd y Baddon, Aberystwyth SY23 2NN

Tel/Ffôn +44 (0) 1970 617998
Fax/Ffacs +44 (0) 1970 611223
Email/Ebost arad.goch@btconnect.com

Artistic Director/Cyfarwyddwr Artistig: **Jeremy Turner**
Administrator/Gweinyddydd: **Annette Davies**

Artistic Policy Polisi Artistig:

To create high-standard and sophisticated, contemporary theatre, primarily for young audiences in Wales; to create links between Wales and other cultures and countries by touring the best of the company's productions abroad and by inviting new work into Wales; to encourage and instigate new ideas and work for theatre for young audiences through co-operation with other artists, companies and organisations.

Darperir theatr gyfoes o'r safon uchaf, yn bennaf i gynulleidfaoedd ifanc yng Nghymru; gweithredir i greu cysylltiadau rhwng Cymru a gwledydd a diwylliannau eraill drwy fynd â'r goreuon o gynhyrchiadau ARAD GOCH dramor a thrwy wahodd artistiaid o dramor i berfformio yng Nghymru; anogir gwaith newydd a datblygir syniadau newydd drwy cydweitho gydag artistiaid, cwmnïau a sefydliadau eraill.

Company History Hanes y Cwmni:

Formed in 1989, ARAD GOCH creates new work primarily for young audiences. The company's repertoire combines both contemporary and traditional source material with a variety of physical and imagistic theatre, contemporary and traditional performance styles and live music. The company creates new work by: commissioning new plays; adapting children's and young people's literature for the stage; devising work with regular groups of performers. The company tours both main-stage productions and small scale, studio productions which are often contained in their own enclosed environments. In 1999 Arad Goch instigated the new performance group LABI, to question the status quo of theatre in Wales and to develop new work by young performers.

ARAD GOCH organises AGOR DRYSAU - OPENING DOORS Wales International Festival of Theatre for Young Audiences.

Ffurfiwyd ym 1989 i greu gwaith newydd yn bennaf i gynulleidfaoedd ifanc. Mae gwaith y cwmni yn cyfuno deunydd cyfoes a traddodiadol ag amrywiaeth o arddulliau perfformio a cherddoriaeth fyw. Creir cynhyrchiadau newydd drwy (i) gomisiynu sgriptiau newydd (ii) addasu llenyddiaeth blant a phobl ifanc at ddefnydd theatrig a (iii) dyfeisio gyda grwpiau o actorion. Mae'r cwmni'n darparu gwaith ar gyfer llwyfannau mawrion ynghŷd â chynyrchiadau llai o faint ar gyfer perfformiadau stiwdio.

"MERCHED Y GERDDI" Photography Keith Morris

Yn 1999 cychwynwyd y grŵp perfformio newydd LABI, o dan ymbarel ARAD GOCH, i gwestiynu'r sefyllfa sydd ohoni yn y theatr yng Ngymru ac i ddatblygu gwaith newydd gan berfformwyr ifanc.

Mae ARAD GOCH yn trefnu AGOR DRYSAU - OPENING DOORS Gŵyl Theatr Ryngwladol Cymru i Gynulleidfaoedd Ifainc.

Special Notes

The scale of the company's work depends on individual productions: some are made for a maximum of 75 children (especially work for very small children) others are performed in middle scale venues.

The company has toured widely abroad including tours to the USA, Canada, Singapore, Sweden and Ireland where it won the prize for the best children's production in the 1996 Dublin International Theatre Festival.

Past Productions Cynhyrchiadau'r Gorffennol:

Productions of note during the last five years:

Taliesin (1996-8); **Over the Stone** (1993-7); **Old Hat** (1998-); **Dilema** (1999-); **The Giant's Daughter** (2000-).

Future Plans Cynlluniau at y dyfodol:

Current and new productions available 2002 onwards:

The Stones/ *Tafliad Carreg;*
Winter Pictures/*Hel Meddyliau;*
Cinio Ysgol, Y Sied;
Moonlit Night/*Lleuad yn Olau.*

Cwmni Ballet Gwent

30 Glasllwch Cresc, Newport, Gwent NP20 3SE

Tel/*Ffôn*   **+44 (0) 1633 253985**
Fax/*Ffacs*   **+44 (0) 1633 221690**
Email/*Ebost*   **dariusjames@welshballet.co.uk**

Artistic Director/*Cyfarwyddwr Artistig*: **Darius Jones**
Administrator/*Gweinyddydd*: **Yvonne Williams**

Artistic Policy Polisi Artistig:

Independent Ballet Wales is a ballet based dance company. It aims to educate and inform people about dance through the performance of accessible and original dance works and through dance workshops open to all.

Company History Hanes y Cwmni:

Cwmni Ballet Gwent was founded in 1986, when the company undertook one performance at Chapter Arts Centre in Cardiff. Building every year on the success of its productions the company now tour to around 100 venues each year with a programme of performances and workshops throughout the UK and Eire.

Creatively, from the period of 1986 to 1990, the company was able to employ the services of top choreographers to add to its repertoire of small scale ballets. Amongst these commissions were ex Royal Ballet dancer Jennifer Jackson, who created *Missing Pieces* for the company in 1989, Ysabelle Taylor, formerly with The Royal Swedish Ballet who created *Heartbeat* in 1988 and Jonathan Burnett, formerly of The Lindsey Kemp Company who created *Villenelle* in 1990.

In 1991, due to funding cuts, Darius James, the company's Artistic Director choreographed *Hiawatha*, the company's first full length work. *Cinderella Mossycoat* followed in 1992, *Beauty and the Beast* in 1993, *The Swan* in 1994, another version of *Cinderella* in 1995, *Red Riding Hood and the Legend of Wolves* in 1996, *A Midsummer Night's Dream* in 1997, *The Tempest* in 1998, *Twelfth Night* in 1999, *As You Like It* and *Giselle Connotation* in 2000, *Romeo + Juliet* on 2001.

In 2002 the company is touring 100s of Arts Centres, theatres and schools with its brand new production of *The Taming of the Shrew*.

Past Productions Cynhyrchiadau'r Gorffennol:

(Productions still in rep)
A Midsummer Night's Dream (1997); **The Tempest** (1998); **Twelfth Night** (1999); **As You Like It; Giselle Connotation** (2000); **Romeo & Juliet** (2001).

Future Plans Cynlluniau at y dyfodol:

The Taming of The Shrew (2002).

Bara Caws

Uned 1A, Cibyn, Caernarfon, LL55 2BD

Tel/Ffôn	**+44 (0) 1286 676335**
Fax/Ffacs	**+44 (0) 1286 671814**
Email/Ebost	**tbaracaw@btconnect.com**

Artistic Director/Cyfarwyddwr Artistig: **Ian Rowlands**
Administrator/Gweinyddydd: **Linda Brown**

Artistic Policy Polisi Artistig:

Bara Caws is the only revenue company funded specifically to tour community theatre in Wales. The main aim of the company is to create relevant theatre of the highest quality for this audience.

Bara Caws yw'r unig cwmni refeniw sy'n cael ei ariannu yn unswydd i deithio theatr i'r gymuned yng Nghymru. Prif nod y cwmni yw i greu theatr o berthnasedd ac o'r safon uchaf ar gyfer y gynulleidfa hon.

Company History Hanes y Cwmni:

Bara Caws is the oldest established professional theatre company in Wales. Since its first show in 1977 the company has staged and toured close to 77 shows. Indeed, some people in Wales say that Bara Caws is Welsh theatre as it has existed for so long and has entertained so many over the years.

Bara Caws yw'r cwmni mwyaf sefydliedig o bob cwmni theatr proffesiynnol yng Nghymru. Ers y sioe gyntaf yn ôl ym 1977, mae'r cwmni wedi llwyfannu a theithio yn agos at 77 o sioeau. Yn wir, i rai bobl yng Nghymru, Bara Caws yw'r theatr Gymraeg am iddi bara cyhyd a diddanu cynifer o bobl dros y blynyddoedd.

NOTES:

Bara Caws is an active member of 'Offspring', a grouping of theatre companies from minority cultures in Europe. Minority cultures can be isolating: Offspring believes that through a dialogue with other cultures it is possible to gain strength by placing one's unique cultural experience in a broader context.

Mae Bara Caws yn aelod blaenllaw o 'Offspring', sef grwp o gwmniau theatr o ddiwylliannau lleiafrifol Ewrop. Gall diwylliannau lleiafrifol fod yn ynysig, ac felly mae Offspring o'r farn mai trwy siarad gyda diwylliannau lleiafrifol eraill mae modd ennyn nerth trwy osod eich diwylliant unigryw eich hun mewn cyd-destun ehangach.

Past Productions Cynhyrchiadau'r Gorffennol:

Hardcore Bethesda Fuzz; Sundance; Al-a-Mo; Paradwys Waed; DJ Faust; Al a Dorothy; Ben Set; Lliwiau Rhyddid; Bingo Bach.

Future Plans Cynlluniau at y dyfodol:

Mwnci Nel; Briwsion o'r gegin (2002); **Y Tywysog Bach** (2003).

"DJ FAUST" Photography Keith Morris

Theatr y Byd

Unit 4, The Maltings, East Tyndall St,
Cardiff CF24 5EZ

Tel/Ffôn   **+44 (0) 29 2049 9122**
Fax/Ffacs   **+44 (0) 29 2049 9122**
                  +44 (0) 29 2045 5320 (evenings)

Artistic Director/Cyfarwyddwr Artistig: **Chris Morgan**
Administrator/Gweinyddydd: **Liz Cowling**
Production Coordinator/Cydlynydd Cynhyrchu: **Dave Roxburgh**

Artistic Policy Polisi Artistig:

Theatr y Byd has been in existence for 10 years and is committed to innovative
productions of new writing.

Company History Hanes y Cwmni:

The company has toured, and continues to tour, throughout Wales and into Ireland,
Scotland, England and France. It receives project funding from the Arts Council of Wales.

Past Productions Cynhyrchiadau'r Gorffennol:

**Inside Out - A portrait of Ivor Novello; Marriage of Convenience;
Pacific, Môr Tawel; New South Wales; Blue Heron in the Womb; Lludw'r
Garreg.**

Future Plans Cynlluniau at y dyfodol:

Further commissions of new writing.

Carlson Dance Company

Chapter, Market Rd, Canton, Cardiff CF5 1QE

Tel/Ffôn	**+44 (0) 1291 635631**
	07971 633 295 mobile
Fax/Ffacs	**+44 (0) 1291 635631**
Email/Ebost	**emmacarlsonwales@hotmail.com**

Artistic Directors/*Cyfarwyddwyr Artistig:* **Emma Carlson, Sally Carlson**
Administrators/*Gweinyddwyr:* **Emma Carlson, Sally Carlson**

Artistic Policy Polisi Artistig:

To create professional dance theatre that communicates effectively to a wide spectrum of the community.
To pursue originality and excellence in all aspects of the Company's work.
To create work that is both entertaining and thought provoking.
The Company's education work aims to provide a safe and creative environment, in which young people from diverse backgrounds can access their own creativity and express themselves in a positive way.

Company History Hanes y Cwmni:

Carlson Dance Company was formed in 1992 by Artistic Directors Emma and Sally Carlson. Prior to this, both performer - choreographer Emma Carlson and designer - director Sally Carlson worked extensively with numerous companies and choreographers in Wales, the UK and Europe. Since its formation the Company has created and toured nine substantial works, most of which have toured throughout the UK and Europe. Venues have included The Place Theatre in London, Chapter Arts in Cardiff, Fabbrica Europa Festival in Florence, Art Berezillia Festival in Kiev and Bluecoat Arts Centre in Liverpool amongst others. The Company's work is suitable for small-mid scale venues. In 1998, the Company set up 'Dance Blast', a unique dance performance scheme for young people aged 11-18. Dance Blast annual participation figures exceed 5,000.

Wacky, wonderful, beautiful and moving, the Carlson sisters' work is a unique mélange of mesmerising dance, quirky humour and cut-throat theatrical absurdity. The Company is artist-led and strives for innovation and excellence. The Carlson sisters' approach to making work often involves collaborating with other artists, such as sonic artist Robert Lippok of Berlin's 'To Rococo Rot' and more recently with Pete Shenton of 'Live Bait'. The Company's portfolio of work can be appreciated on many different levels, as sheer enjoyable entertainment, as accomplished performance and as thought provoking and serious 'high art'. Therefore, it is suitable for a diverse audience. Carlson Dance Company is unique to Wales as its activities encompass both the creation of original professional dance theatre and the delivery of a substantial dance education scheme.
Co-Artistic Director Emma Carlson has recently graduated with a Masters Degree in choreography with performing arts at Middlesex University in London.

Past Productions Cynhyrchiadau'r Gorffennol:

Midnight Zone; LDX; Decay; Pantechnicon; So Far Suite; Terminal.

Future Plans Cynlluniau at y dyfodol:

The Company is combining its professional performance practice with specially choreographed work created with local young people to be presented alongside the production.

The Company plans a further tour of Terminal in autumn 2002, and to create a new production available for touring in spring 2003. The Company's Dance Blast education scheme is also set to expand and develop over the next few years.

Photography Paul Jeff

Clwyd Theatr Cymru

Mold, Flintshire, CH7 1YA

Tel/Ffôn   **+44 (0) 1352 756331** administration
    +44 (0) 1352 756114 box office
Fax/Ffacs   **+44 (0) 1352 701558**
Email/Ebost   **mail@clwyd-theatr-cymru.co.uk**
Web/Y Wê   **www.clwyd-theatr-cymru.co.uk**

Director/Cyfarwyddwr: **Terry Hands**
Associate Director/Cyfarwyddwr Cyswllt: **Tim Baker**
General Manager/Rheolwraig Gyffredinol: **Chris Ricketts**
Financial Controller/Rheolwraig Cyllid: **Julia Grime**
Production Manager/Rheolwr Cynhyrchu: **Bob Irwin**
Marketing Manager/Rheolwraig Marchnata: **Ann Williams**
Sponsorship Manager/Rheolwraig Nawdd: **Annie Dayson**
Technical-Development Manager/Rheolwr Technegol a Datblygu: **Pat Nelder**
Associate Director Plays & Touring/Cyfarwyddwr Cyswllt Dramâu a Theithio: **William James**

Artistic Policy Polisi Artistig:

To become the local theatre for every town in Wales. To establish the highest possible standards of production and performance. To serve as a research, training and development centre for present and future generations of Welsh theatre practitioners. To provide a focus for drama in the North Wales region.

To extend that provision across Wales and develop a new audience by touring, marketing, TIE/YPT and by establishing artistic collaborations, particularly with the capital. To create an identity and establish a profile that will enable Clwyd Theatr Cymru to become a national asset with an international reputation. To collaborate with the ACW in maintaining and increasing interest in drama throughout Wales.

Company History/ Hanes y Cwmni:

Created through the vision of Clwyd County Council and its Chief Executive Haydn Rees, the theatre was opened in 1976. Located a mile from Mold town centre the building incorporates five performance venues: The Anthony Hopkins Theatre, Emlyn Williams Theatre, Studio 2, multi-function Clwyd Room and Cinema. Terry Hands accepted the post of Director on 2 May 1997. The name changed to Clwyd Theatr Cymru in 1998 to reflect the theatre's new identity and remit following the changes brought about by local government reorganisation in Wales. In 1998 the theatre won the Barclays/TMA Theatre of the Year award and in 1999 was designated a Welsh National Performing Arts Company by the Arts Council of Wales.

Wedi ei chreu trwy weledigaeth Cyngor Sir Clwyd a'i Phrif Weithredwr Haydn Rees, agorwyd y theatr ym 1976. A'i lleoliad filltir o ganol tref Yr Wyddgrug, mae'r adeilad yn gyfuniad o bum man perfformio: Theatr Anthony Hopkins, Theatr Emlyn Williams, Stiwdio 2, Ystafell Clwyd aml-weithredol a'r Sinema.
Derbyniodd Terry Hands ei swydd Cyfarwyddwr ar Mai 2 1997.
Newidiodd yr enw i Clwyd Theatr Cymru yn 1998 i adlewyrchu hunaniaeth newydd a chyfrifoldeb y theatr yn dilyn newidiadau a ddaeth wedi ad-drefnu llywodraeth leol yng Nghymru. Yn 1998 enillodd y theatr wobr Barclays/TMA Theatr y Flwyddyn ac yn 1999 cafodd ei phenodi yn Gwmni Celfyddydau Perfformio Cenedlaethol Cymreig gan Gyngor Celfyddydau Cymru.

Past Productions Cynhyrchiadau'r Gorffennol:

Equus; Abigail's Party; Rape of the Fair Country; Afore Night Come; A Christmas Carol; Cinderella; The Journey of Mary Kelly; Sweeney Todd - The Demon Barber of Fleet Street (1997-98)**; Dead Funny; Blue Remembered Hills; Celf 'Art'; Gaslight; They Offered Bob and Wilma Cash; The Norman Conquests: Table Manners, Living Together, Round & Round The Garden; Of Mice And Men; Aladdin - The Wok 'N' Roll Panto; Hosts Of Rebecca** (1998-99)**; Happy End; Twelfth Night; Song Of The Earth; Macbeth; An Evening With Charles Dickens; Dick Whittington And The Coolest Cat In Town; Under Milk Wood; The Threepenny Opera; Flora's War** (1999-00)**; Hard Times; Damwain a Hap** (Cyfieithiad newydd o Accidental Death Of An Anarchist)**; Private Lives; Cinderella - The Panto With Soul; King Lear** (2000-01)**; Bedroom Farce; Accidental Death of an Anarchist; To Kill a Mockingbird** (2001-02).

Future Plans/ Cynlluniau at y dyfodol:

Under Milkwood; The Rabbit; Jack & the Beanstalk; Rosencrantz and Guilderstern are Dead (2001-02).

"KING LEAR"
Directed by Terry Hands,
Photography Ivan Kyncl

Clwyd Theatr Cymru
Theatre for Young People /
Theatr i Bobl Ifanc

Mold, Flintshire CH7 1YA

Tel/Ffôn **+44 (0) 1352 756331**
Fax/Ffacs **+44 (0) 1352 758323**
Email/Ebost **education@clwyd-theatr-cymru.co.uk**
Web/Y Wê **www.clwyd-theatr-cymru.co.uk**

Artistic Director (Young People's Theatre)
/Cyfarwyddwr Artistig (Theatr i Bobl Ifanc): **Tim Baker**
Administrator/Gweinyddydd: **David Greenhalgh**

Artistic Policy Polisi Artistig:

To produce challenging and innovative theatre projects for young people which both excite them about theatre and inspire debate, contributing to their education through theatre. To create workshops and other supporting events for young people. CTC TYP works bilingually (Welsh/English) and has a particular interest in collaborations with other minority language organisations.

Rydym yn creu cynyrchiadau theatrig newydd a heriol ar gyfer pobl ifanc. Ein nôd yw cyflwyno theatr gyffrous a dadleuol a fydd yn cyfrannu at eu haddysg trwy theatr. Rydym hefyd yn creu gweithdai a digwyddiadau cefnogol eraill ar gyfer pobl ifanc. Mae gan TBI CTC ddiddordeb arbennig mewn cyd-weithio gyda sefydliadau ieithoedd lleiafrifol eraill.

Company History Hanes y Cwmni:

Annual contact with over 30,000 young people. Regular programme of new plays and adaptations for primary and secondary pupils. Clwyd Theatr Cymru - Theatre for Young People's policy is to bring young people to a theatre space, rather than tour to schools.

Cyswllt blynyddol gyda dros 30,00 o bobl ifanc. Rhaglen flynyddol o ddramâu ac addasiadau newydd ar gyfer disgyblion ysgolion cynradd ac uwchradd. Ein polisi yw i ddod â phobl ifanc i'r theatr, yn hytrach na theithio i ysgolion.

Past Productions Cynhyrchiadau'r Gorffennol:

The Changelings; Flora's War/Rhyfel Flora; Of Mice and Men, Word for Word/Gair am Air; Hard Times; The Secret; To Kill a Mockingbird.

Future Plans Cynlluniau at y dyfodol:

A trilogy of plays for 9-11 year olds
A collaboration on a GCSE set text with Clwyd Theatr Cymru main house
An international project for young people

Trioleg o ddramâu ar gyfer plant 9-11 oed
Cyd-brosiect ar destun gosod TGAU gyda'r prif theatr (Clwyd Theatr Cymru)
Prosiect rhyngwladol ar gyfer pobl ifanc

"FLORA'S WAR" Directed by Tim Baker

Diversions

The Dance Company of Wales

Studio 18, Tyndall St, PO Box 1028,
Cardiff CF10 4XJ

Tel/Ffôn	**+44 (0) 29 2046 5345**
Fax/Ffacs	**+44 (0) 29 2046 5346**
Email/Ebost	**diversions@diversionsdance.co.uk**
Web/Y Wê	**www.diversionsdance.co.uk**

Artistic Director/Cyfarwyddwr Artistig: **Roy Campbell-Moore**
Administrator/Gweinyddydd: **Jocelyn Elmer**

Artistic Policy Polisi Artistig:

Diversions is a Wales National Performing Arts Company with a national remit and a commitment to excellence and access.

Core work is commissioning dance from international choreographers which is performed alongside the work of Artistic Director Roy Campbell-Moore. The Company tours across Wales and the UK, performing in venues as diverse as national touring houses and community halls. It has toured internationally to Latvia, Australia, Slovenia, Ecuador, Japan and Russia.

Diversions' extensive education and training programme includes an 'Artists in Education' programme, which delivers workshops to schools, colleges and community groups. The Company holds summer schools and residential courses; runs an Associates Scheme; and hosts dance apprenticeships. Diversions also produces a wide variety of new work often in partnership with touring agencies and venues, including work by Wales based choreographers, foreign dance companies, films and community projects.

Company History Hanes y Cwmni:

In 1983, Roy Campbell-Moore and Ann Sholem created Diversions. Since then, the Company has grown to a team of eight dancers and seven staff. In 1999, the Company was awarded the status of a Wales National Performing Arts Company.

Future Plans Cynlluniau at y dyfodol:

In 2005, Diversions will become a resident organisation at the Wales Millennium Centre in Cardiff Bay along with eight other companies including Welsh National Opera, Urdd Gobaith Cymru, the Wales Amateur Music Federation, Hijinx Theatre Company, the Touch Trust and Academi. Facilities for Diversions will include an international-quality production studio, a second studio and administration, technical and wardrobe spaces. Collaborative projects with the other resident organisations are currently in planning for the next 3 years.

"CLEARING"
Choreographer Zvi Gotheiner
Photography David Lee

Earthfall

Chapter, Market Rd, Canton, Cardiff CF5 1QE

Tel/Ffôn	**+44 (0) 29 2022 1314**
Fax/Ffacs	**+44 (0) 29 2034 2259**
Email/Ebost	**earthfall@earthfall.org.uk**
Web/Y Wê	**www.earthfall.org.uk**

Artistic Directors/Cyfarwyddwyr Artistig: **Jim Ennis / Jessica Cohen**
Administrative Director/Cyfarwyddwr Gweinyddol: **Alison Woods**

Artistic Policy Polisi Artistig:

Since forming in 1989, Earthfall have evolved a distinctive and challenging methodology for rehearsal and performance. Broadly speaking, the company are concerned with addressing the relationship that exists between performer and audience. It's a concern strengthened by the company's rare ability to bring political and social agendas into an arena commonly limited by accepted definitions of what dance is and what it can be.

The overriding concern is always to look at what can be said physically and emotionally within set limitations, sometimes of the body's own making, sometimes through the content of the piece. It's the detail, as always in Earthfall's works, which speaks volumes and which has helped make the company not only Wales' leading exponent of dance theatre, but one of Europe's most sought after companies.

Company History Hanes y Cwmni:

Earthfall was formed in 1989 by Jessica Cohen and Jim Ennis with a policy of forging radical choreography with live music and strong visual imagery. The company rapidly established itself as an outstanding exponent of pioneering dance theatre. Earthfall's issue-based work is concerned with seeking a personal honesty, passion and economy in physical performance to produce quality work of depth. Earthfall has performed throughout the world in many major festivals and has featured on numerous TV and Radio broadcasts. The company has received several awards for its live performance and film work, most recently the Bafta Cymru Award winner for Best Short Film for Too Old To Dream.

Past Productions Cynhyrchiadau'r Gorffennol:

Earthfall (1989); **Nomads** (1990); **The Secret Soul of Things, ... Our Lives Brief as Photos** (1991); **The Intimate Jig, Intimate Jig (film short C4)** (1992); **i and i; Girl Standing by the Lake** (1994); **forever and ever, You to Remember (film)** (1995); **Fabulous Wounds, Too Old to Dream** (BAFTA winner) (1997-98); **Rococo Blood** (1999-2000); **aD** (2001).

Future Plans Cynlluniau at y dyfodol:

New work, 'I Can't Stand Up for Falling Down' based on the turbulent history of an extended family, touring Wales, UK and Europe from Autumn 2002 as part of Earthfall's House Project. A site locational work follows in 2003 and 2004.

"ROCOCO BLOOD"
Photography Hugo Glendinning

Eddie Ladd

Maesglas, Tremain, Aberteifi SA43 1RR

Tel/*Ffôn* **07974 394415**
Email/*Ebost* **eddie@dybli.fsnet.co.uk**

Artistic Director/*Cyfarwyddwr Artistig:* **Eddie Ladd**
Administrator/*Gweinyddydd:* **Eddie Ladd**

Artistic Policy Polisi Artistig:

Making Welsh work in Wales and touring it everywhere.
Creu gwaith cymreig yng Nghymru a'i deithio i bobman.

Company History Hanes y Cwmni:

Started to make solo work at the beginning of the 90s whilst at the same time performing with Brith Gof.

Past Productions Cynhyrchiadau'r Gorffennol:

Callas sings mad songs (1993); **Unglucklicherweise** (1994); **Once upon a time in the west** (1996); **Lla'th** (1998); **Scarface** (2000).

Future Plans Cynlluniau at y dyfodol:

The next 2 years will focus on making web-based productions but with some live performances.
Creu gwaith ar y we yw'r cynllun am y ddwy flynedd nesa ond yn dal i berfformio'n fyw hefyd.

Elan Wales

Chapter, Market Rd, Canton, Cardiff CF5 1QE

Tel/*Ffôn*	**+44 (0) 29 2034 5831**
Fax/*Ffacs*	**+44 (0) 29 2034 5831**
Email/*Ebost*	**info@elan-wales.fsnet.co.uk**
Web/*Y Wê*	**www.elanw.demon.co.uk**

Artistic Director/*Cyfarwyddwr Artistig*: **Firenza Guidi**
Administrators/*Gweinyddwyr*: **David Murray, Cecilia Mantelassi**

Artistic Policy Polisi Artistig:

Elan is a performance training, research and production company creating projects which enable and encourage collaborations between performers and artists from different parts of Wales, Europe and beyond in the belief that there is a language, in theatre, which unifies without abolishing differences. Elan's desire is to provide the initial means and inspiration for the people of a community - as well as for professional artists - not only to discover and use their creative power, but also to continue to develop it if they wish to do so.

Elan aims to:

Reclaim a place for theatre in the lives of people as a rightful and irreplaceable space for memory, history, culture, the search for individual and collective identity. Bring together academics and practitioners, intellectuals and artists to create a dialogue between theatre theory and practice. Bridge the gap between 'high art' and 'community' events. Establish a true and dynamic dialogue between different performative languages such as music, movement, singing and vocal work, text, plastic and visual arts. Motivate performers' self-exploration and development by providing the company with a framework of on-going training and continuous challenges. Propose and implement the practice of training as empowerment. Create long-standing collaborations which continue to flourish in time and across boundaries.

Company History Hanes y Cwmni:

Created in 1989 by Firenza Guidi and David Murray, Elan is committed to creating new work in the form of site-specific, video, installation, high-quality, highly visual, small and large-scale performances/events in unusual and unexplored locations. Elan's unique formula of the performance/montage has proved a powerful and extremely adaptable vehicle for presentation and performance training at both professional and community level, as well as a means of establishing long-standing collaborations.

Past Productions Cynhyrchiadau'r Gorffennol:

Cybermama; State of Grace 1/Stato di Grazia 1 (1999); **In My Mouth; State of Grace 2/Stato di Grazia 2; Bytes; Transit Sheds; Metamorfosi; Faust; R.ex** (2000).

Future Plans Cynlluniau at y dyfodol:

Elan continues to build upon and expand its unique programme of performance training throughout Wales and beyond.

They are currently organising their next large-scale, four-phase project with transnational partners under the European Culture 2001 Programme.

"R. ex" Photography Keith Morris

Equilibre

Carreg Dressage, Abercegir, Machynlleth,
Powys SY20 8NW

Tel/Ffôn   **+44 (0) 1650 511222**
Fax/Ffacs   **+44 (0) 1650 511800**
Email/Ebost **jlf@equilibre.co.uk**
Web/Y Wê   **www.equilibre.co.uk**

Artistic Directors/Cyfarwyddwyr Artistig:
Our work is the collaboration of all members of the company.
Led by/Arweinwyr: **Jane Lloyd Francis, Georges Dewez,**
Musical Director/Cyfarwyddwr Cerddorol: **Jez Danks**
Administrator/Gweinyddydd: **Jane Lloyd Francis**

Artistic Policy Polisi Artistig:

To create a startling and memorable fusion of physical choreographies involving horses, humans, music, and visual arts.

Company History Hanes y Cwmni:

Established in 1993 to explore the possibilities of presenting elements of classical riding in an extravagant theatrical context of integrated devised spectacle.

Past Productions Cynhyrchiadau'r Gorffennol:

Khazar explored themes of dream travel and dream reading where shadowy moments of revelation unfolded before your eyes.

Revolution was a richly costumed opulent production investigating the place of the great riders and other characters of the European courts in the 17th and 18th centuries.

The Horse, our latest production, interpreted Ronald Duncan's poem of the same name, presenting magnificent working shires in contrast to the fiery agility of Iberian stallions in the context of work, war and grace.

Future Plans Cynlluniau at y dyfodol:

To continue to develop and refine a form of collaborative theatrical event, combining equine and human performances which are unique in Britain.

"LUSITANO STALLION: GAUCHO" Photography Mike Evans

Cwmni'r Frân Wen

Yr Hen Ysgol Gynradd, Ffordd Pentraeth,
Porthaethwy, Ynys Môn LL59 5HS

Tel/Ffôn   **+44 (0) 1248 715048**
Fax/Ffacs   **+44 (0) 1248 715225**
Email/Ebost **CwmniFranWen@aol.com**

Artistic Director/Cyfarwyddwr Artistig: **Iola Ynyr**
Administrator/Gweinyddydd: **Nia Rees Williams**

Artistic Policy Polisi Artistig:

Our intention is to present exciting theatre of the highest standard, which promotes the curiosity of the audience and which encourages young people themselves to participate in theatrical activities. Our goal is to use the power of theatre to shake the audiences emotionally and to make them look at their world anew.

Ein bwriad yw darparu theatr gyffrous o'r safon uchaf sydd yn creu chwilfrydedd yn y gynulleidfa ac yn arwain pobl ifanc i fentro o'u gwirfodd i gyfranogi mewn digwyddiadau theatrig. Ein nod yw defnyddio pwer y theatr i ysgwyd y gynulleidfa yn emosiynol a'u hysgogi i edrych ar y byd o'r newydd.

Company History Hanes y Cwmni:

Frân Wen was established in 1984 as part of Coleg Harlech's Arts Centre, to provide theatre in education to schools in the then county of Gwynedd. The philosophy from the very beginning was to present, in the Welsh language, a quality theatrical experience to classes of school children to be used as an educational resource.

The company receives support from Gwynedd Council, Ynys Môn County Council, Conwy Borough Council and the Arts Council of Wales.

In July 1995 the company moved to the old primary school in Porthaethwy (Menai Bridge). As a result the company is in an excellent geographical position to service all of the new local authorities in its area.

Sefydlwyd Cwmni'r Frân Wen yn 1984 fel rhan o ganolfan y Celfyddydau yng Ngholeg Harlech er mwyn darparu prosiectau Theatr mewn Addysg i Ysgolion Gwynedd fel y'i adwaenwyd ar y pryd. Yr athroniaeth o'r cychwyn cyntaf oedd cyflwyno profiad theatrig safonol i ddosbarth o ddisgyblion ar y tro i'w ddefnyddio fel anodd addysgol a hynny trwy gyfrwng y Gymraeg.

Mae'r Cwmni yn derbyn nawdd gan Gyngor Sir Gwynedd, Cyngor Sir Ynys Môn, Cyngor Bwrdeistref Conwy a Chyngor Celfyddydau Cymru.

Symudodd y Cwmni ym mis Gorffennaf 1995 i'r Hen Ysgol Gynradd ym Mhorthaethwy. O ganlyniad i'r symud mae'r Cwmni mewn sefyllfa daearyddol hwylus i wasanaethu'r awdurdodau newydd.

Past Productions Cynhyrchiadau'r Gorffennol:

Cae o Adar Duon / The Field of Blackbirds; Snog Sbar; Lleisiau yn y Parc; Y Sgam.

Future Plans Cynlluniau at y dyfodol:

Developing our work in the community, through both Welsh and English.

Datblygu gwaith cymunedol y Cwmni a hynny drwy gyfrwng y Gymraeg a'r Saesneg.

"CAE O ADAR DUON / THE FIELD OF BLACKBIRDS" Photography Keith Morris

Good Cop Bad Cop

c/o 418 Cowbridge Rd East, Canton,
Cardiff CF5 1JL

Tel/*Ffôn* **+44 (0) 29 2040 5770**
Email/*Ebost* **neudniddeud@hotmail.com**

Artistic Directors/*Cyfarwyddwyr Artistig:* **Richard Huw-Morgan**
John Rowley
Paul Jeff

Artistic Policy Polisi Artistig:

Good Cop Bad Cop is a performance company specialising in theatre of irrevocable acts, a form of structured, restageable performances designed to re-fertilise barren auditoria and non-theatrical spaces with an irreverent disrespect for convention and taste. Though restageable, Good Cop Bad Cop events are unrepeatable and inevitably involve the reappropriation or reorientation of an existing 'art' event, sometimes our own.

Company History Hanes y Cwmni:

Good Cop Bad Cop was formed in 1995 by performers John Rowley and Richard Huw-Morgan who had previously worked together in Brith Gof and as Das Wunden. The inclusion of photographer Paul Jeff and a variety of collaborating practitioners from visual, sound and performance backgrounds gave rise to the name change and a diversification into other artistic fields. Having taken a break from collaborating since 1998, 2001 sees the return of the three renaissance men as a unique artistic force to be reckoned with.

Past Productions Cynhyrchiadau'r Gorffennol:

Productions as Das Wunden
18:40 20:40; Would you like to come to my room? (1993); **Caucus; This is Caucus too** (1994); **Das Wunden - the gig; Caucus 3** (1995).

Performances as Good Cop Bad Cop

The White Room (1995); **Closing Down Sale** (1996); **Loop** (1998); **Homeopathic Pornography** (2000).

Future Plans Cynlluniau at y dyfodol:

Good Shop Bad Shop; Last man standing; Mysteries; People who live in glass houses ...

Photography Sian Trenberth

Green Ginger

32 The Norton, Tenby SA70 8AB

Tel/Ffôn   **+44 (0) 117 9225599**
Fax/Ffacs   **+44 (0) 117 9225599**
Email/Ebost   **mail@greenginger.net**

Artistic Directors/Cyfarwyddwyr Artistig: **Terry Lee, Chris Pirie**
Administrator/Gweinyddydd: **Chris Pirie**

Artistic Policy Polisi Artistig:

Green Ginger is celebrating two decades of touring high quality, low language theatre productions all over the planet, maintaining a global reputation at the cutting edge of accessible, original theatre.

Educational workshops in all of the company's varied skills are also available.

Company History Hanes y Cwmni:

Terry Lee began street performing with InterAction before working with Barry Smith, ITV's Spitting Image and as manipulator on several Jim Henson/Frank Oz films. Designer and maker Chris Pirie joined in 1986, having cut his teeth with Industrial & Domestic Theatre Contractors. In 1997, Terry's brother-outlaw James Osborne left a comfortable career in the hotel trade to join Green Ginger as its short-suffering technician. John Barber and Billy Paul joined the company at the start of production of Green Ginger's latest touring creation, BAMBI The Wilderness Years.

Working with mime / physical theatre directors such as Dante Agostini, John Lee, Luci Gorrel Barnes, Kevin Brooking and Bim Mason has ensured a repertoire of versatile, low-language street and theatre shows with a mind-watering sense of nonsense, and a place "… at the forefront of the revolution in British puppetry".

Past Productions Cynhyrchiadau'r Gorffennol:

TERRY LEE solo shows
Herschel and the Beast; A Television Show; Mack the Giant Thriller; The Last Resort; The Story So Far (1978-86).
GREEN GINGER shows
Gaston & Pedro; Madame Zero; Frank Einstein; Boris the Eurobot; PRATs; Slaphead; BAMBI (1987-2000).

Future Plans Cynlluniau at y dyfodol:

Touring BAMBI and our Street Theatre shows around the world throughout 2001-02. Further collaborations with Welsh National Opera, teaching at Welsh College of Music and Drama and École Supérieure de la Marionnette (France). New production: "Coming Soon" 15 minute commission for Petit Bazar Erotik festival, touring to Belgium and France.

Gwent Theatre

The Drama Centre, Pen y Pound, Abergavenny, Monmouthshire NP7 5UD

Tel/*Ffôn*   **+44 (0) 1873 853167**
Fax/*Ffacs*   **+44 (0) 1873 853910**
Email/*Ebost* **gwenttie@aol.com**
Web/*Y Wê*   **www.gwenttie.co.uk**

Artistic Director/*Cyfarwyddwr Artistig:* **Gary Meredith**
Administrator/*Gweinyddydd:* **Julia Davies**

Artistic Policy Polisi Artistig:

Gwent Theatre provides a high quality professional theatre in education and youth theatre service for schools and communities. Productions, performances and workshops create access and participation for young people to experience live theatre and to develop an appreciation of literature and the performing arts, provoke discussion of current issues and inspire an interest in the world in which they live.

The nature of the company's work is all inclusive and contributes to the development of an interest in our cultural heritage and the diversity of the world around us through performances, workshops and youth theatre activities designed to complement local initiatives and strategies.

Company History Hanes y Cwmni:

Gwent Theatre was established in 1976. Based at the Melville Theatre at the Drama Centre, Abergavenny, a well resourced intimate theatre providing rehearsal and performance facilities for the company, the youth theatre and small scale touring companies.

Past Productions Cynhyrchiadau'r Gorffennol:

Mirad, a Boy from Bosnia; Sonia and the Dancing Bear.

Future Plans Cynlluniau at y dyfodol:

Common Threads; Voice; A Spell of Cold Weather.

"MIRAD, A BOY FROM BOSNIA"
Gary Meredith & Jain Boon

Cwmni Theatr Gwynedd

Ffordd Deiniol, Bangor, Gwynedd LL57 2TL

Tel/Ffôn   **+44 (0) 1248 351707**
Fax/Ffacs   **+44 (0) 1248 351915**
Email/Ebost **theatr@theatrgwynedd.co.uk**
Web/Y Wê   **www.theatrgwynedd.com**

Artistic Director/*Cyfarwyddwr Artistig*: **Ian Rowlands**
Administrator Director/*Cyfarwyddwr Gweinyddol*: **Dafydd Thomas**

Artistic Policy Polisi Artistig:

The aim of the company is to dedicate itself to presenting stage works of the highest quality in the Welsh language.

As well as producing current and classic dramas in Welsh we are awake to the need for new work in Welsh and for translations of new work and classics from other languages and cultures.

We aim to create a nucleus of artists and authors which will elevate theatre in Welsh to new heights.

Nod Cwmni Theatr Gwynedd yw ymroi i gyflwyno gwaith llwyfan o'r radd flaenaf yn yr iaith Gymraeg.

Ar wahan i gyflwyno drama gyfoes a chlasurol yn y Gymraeg, rydym yn effro i'r angen mawr sydd am waith newydd yn yr iaith ac am gyfieithiadau o glasuron hen a chyfoes o wledydd eraill er mwyn diwallu'r anghenion.

Bwriedir amcanu at greu nythaid o artistiaid ac awduron fydd yn codi'r ddrama Gymraeg i dir uchel newydd.

Company History Hanes y Cwmni:

Cwmni Theatr Gwynedd was established in 1986 with the support of the Arts Council of Wales and Gwynedd County Council. On average three plays are produced each year and most of them tour to venues throughout Wales, both large and small. Actors and crew are employed as needed, and the company can draw on the permanent staff employed at Theatr Gwynedd.

Because of the shortage of space within Theatr Gwynedd itself we do not have rehearsal space. Over the years we have presented many different types of drama, including the Welsh classics, translations of international classics and many new plays. Throughout the years Cwmni Theatr Gwynedd has offered workshops to schools and colleges based on the current production.

Sefydlwyd Cwmni Theatr Gwynedd ym 1986 gyda chefnogaeth Cyngor Celfyddydau Cymru a Chyngor Sir Gwynedd. Cyflwynir tri chynhyrchiad y flwyddyn ar gyfartaledd ac mae'r rhan fwyaf ohonynt yn teithio i ganolfannau led-led Cymru; y rhai prif ffrwd i'r prif theatrau a'r cynyrchiadau llai eu maint i leoliadau eraill. Cyflogir actorion, technegwyr, rheolwyr llwyfan a chynllunwyr yn ôl y galw; hefyd mae staff parhaol Theatr Gwynedd; technegwyr a'r staff marchnata a gweinyddol yn gweithio i'r Cwmni yn ogystal ag i'r Theatr. Oherwydd diffyg gofod yn Theatr Gwynedd ei hun, nid oes gennym ystafelloedd ymarfer. Dros y blynyddoedd rydym wedi cyflwyno gwahanol fathau o ddrama, megis; y clasuron Cymraeg; cyfieithiadau o glasuron y theatr ryngwladol a hefyd llawer o waith ysgrifennu newydd. Drwy gydol y blynyddoedd bu Cwmni Theatr Gwynedd trwy'r Cyfarwyddwr perthnasol yn cynnig gweithdai i ysgolion uwchradd a cholegau yn seiledig ar y dramâu dan sylw.

Past Productions Cynhyrchiadau'r Gorffennol:

Bownsars; Ffrwd Ceinwen; Wal; Plant Gladys; Comin Jac; Diwedd y Byd; Amadeus; Dynes ddela' Leenane.

Future Plans Cynlluniau at y dyfodol:

Crincod; *an adaptation of Roald Dahl's 'The Twits" (2002).*

Y Gymraes

8 Rhes Penglais, Aberystwyth SY23 2ET

Tel/*Ffôn* **+44 (0) 1970 625347**
Email/*Ebost* **adf@aber.ac.uk**

Artistic Director/*Cyfarwyddwr Artistig:* **Sêra Moore Williams**
Administrator/*Gweinyddydd:* **Andy Freeman**

Artistic Policy Polisi Artistig:

To make and present new text based theatre with a wide relevance, from a Welsh woman's perspective
To experiment with text and form
To challenge both performers and audience
To work when inspired!

I greu a chyflwyno gwaith newydd wedi'i seilio ar destun, gyda pherthnasedd eang, o safbwynt cymraes
I arbrofi gyda thestun a ffurf
I gyflwyno her i berfformwyr ac i gynulleidfa
I weithio pan fo'r yr awen yn gryf!

Past Productions Cynhyrchiadau'r Gorffennol:

Byth Rhy Hwyr (Never To Late); Trais Tyner (Tender Violence); Mae Sian yn Gadael Cymru (Sian is leaving Wales); Mefus (Strawberries); Môr Forwyn (Mermaid); Mab (Son).

Photography Andy Freeman

Hijinx Theatre

Bay Chambers, West Bute St,
Cardiff CF10 5BB

Tel/Ffôn   **+44 (0) 29 2030 0331** general enquiries
Fax/Ffacs   **+44 (0) 29 2030 0332**
Email/Ebost   **info@hijinx.org.uk**
Web/Y Wê   **www.hijinx.org.uk**

Artistic Director/*Cyfarwyddwr Artistig*: **Gaynor Lougher**
Administrative Director/*Cyfarwyddwr Gweinyddol*: **Val Hill**
Associate Director/*Cyfarwyddwr Cyswllt*: **Chris Morgan**

Artistic Policy Polisi Artistig:

Hijinx is an award-winning theatre company taking professional theatre to
communities throughout Wales and England. The company is Wales' leading
small-scale and community touring theatre company and is renowned for
producing exciting, entertaining and accessible new plays.

Hijinx is committed to produce high quality plays with a strong emphasis on
new writing and the fusion of performance, design and music.

To tour to community venues throughout Wales and England providing access to
high quality theatre to communities for whom theatre is not easily accessible
either through geographical, social, cultural or financial constraints.

To create and tour theatre for people with learning disabilities.

To create an inclusive environment by encouraging integration of people with
disabilities in all areas of the company's work.

To create enriching opportunities for artists, participants and audiences by using
flexible, challenging and imaginative approaches to our work.

To undertake rigorous research and evaluation of each project to develop new
audiences whilst nurturing existing ones.

To create a positive and co-operative working environment in which people's
opinions and experience will be valued.

To create an organisation which exemplifies best practice in serving its staff,
associates, participants and audiences, and respects the diversity of individuals and
communities.

Hijinx are committed to new writing.

Hijinx also create productions for people with learning disabilities and tour into day
centres, Gateway clubs, theatres and community venues in Wales and England

In 1999 Hijinx set up Odyssey Theatre, a participatory group for members of the
local community some of whom have learning disabilities; this is funded by an ACW
Lottery A4A grant. The group meet once a week and stage regular productions.

Company History Hanes y Cwmni:

The company was established in 1981 to take high quality professional theatre
to communities who do not normally have access to such an experience.

Since then the company has commissioned over 17 new plays and taken them
to diverse community venues and theatres all over Wales and England. The
company's touring patterns have changed since the early 80s, and while touring
to community venues is still at the core of the company's work, Hijinx also tour
to small-scale and mid-scale venues in England and Wales.

Past Productions Cynhyrchiadau'r Gorffennol:

A Room of my Own; All The Sundays of May (1998)**; Paul
Robeson Knew my Father** (1999)**; Out of Fear; Tarzanne-Queen of
the Valley** (2000)**; To Have and To Hold; Ill Met By Moonlight**
(2001)**.**

Odyssey Theatre Productions:
New Dreams for Old (1999)**; The Other Robinson Crusoe;
Cinderella, Cinderella** (2000)**; Midsummers Nights Dreamers; Peter
Pan & Wendy** (2001)**.**

"TARZANNE - QUEEN OF THE VALLEY" by Greg Cullen Photography Brian Tarr

India Dance Wales

22 Maes-y-Coed, Heath, Cardiff CF14 4HF

Tel/Ffôn   **+44 (0) 29 2034 1239**
Fax/Ffacs   **+44 (0) 29 2034 1239**
Email/Ebost **indiadancewales@hotmail.com**

Artistic Director/Cyfarwyddwr Artistig: **Kiran Ratna**

Artistic Policy Polisi Artistig:

The only professional organisation in Wales for Indian Dance, India Dance Wales work primarily in the Bharatantyam style. The company's aim is to maintain the authenticity and beauty of a classical dance form whilst exploring contemporary ideas and crossing cultural boundaries. Examples include the performance of ancient Sanskrit Plays and Indian Mythology, working in collaboration with the National Museum upon the discovery of some precious Indian Paintings and adapting the Mabinogion and Shakespeare. The company produces and tours accessible and good quality work, dance training and community and education workshops.

Company History Hanes y Cwmni:

India Dance Wales was formerly known as Kiran Ratna in 1993 when its namesake was working as a solo performer; since then the company has worked on a number of challenging and innovative projects with a variety of different dance practitioners. In 1998 the company became formalised as India Dance Wales.

Past Productions Cynhyrchiadau'r Gorffennol:

Myths and Dance (1993); **Shakuntala** ancient Sanskrit play (1994); **Navarasas** Nine Emotions (1995); **Mahabahrita Mabinogion** (1996); **Kalighat Icons** (1999); **Puranic Visions** (2000); **The Tempest** (2001).

Future Plans Cynlluniau at y dyfodol:

Touring **The Tempest**. Awaiting an 'Arts for All' lottery bid which will allow the company to develop its Indian dance training (now that Bharatanatyam has received official recognition and grading from the ISTD) and long-term schools residencies.

"THE TEMPEST" Photography Laura Woods

Theatr Iolo

The Old School Building, Cefn Rd, Mynachdy,
Cardiff CF14 3HS

Tel/Ffôn **+44 (0) 29 2061 3782**
Fax/Ffacs **+44 (0) 29 2052 2225**
Email/Ebost **admin@theatriolo.com**
Web/Y Wê **www.theatriolo.com**

Artistic Director/Cyfarwyddwr Artistig: **Kevin Lewis**
Administrator/Gweinyddydd: **Dolly Schwenk**

Artistic Policy Polisi Artistig:

Creating vibrant theatre for young people to stir the imagination, inspire the heart and challenge the mind.

The company creates performance projects and residencies for young people including those with Special Educational Needs.

Company History Hanes y Cwmni:

Funded by Arts Council of Wales with additional funding from Cardiff County Council, THEATR IOLO has toured to schools in South Wales since 1987. In recent years the company has performed at festivals and venues in Austria, Ireland, England and Wales.

Past Productions Cynhyrchiadau'r Gorffennol:

Days with Frog and Toad; Telling Tales; Something Rich and Strange; The Lost Boys; Stringman; Box of Secrets; Marcos.

Future Plans Cynlluniau at y dyfodol:

Mole in a Hole; The Room; Open Up; Journey; Bison & Sons.

"DAY WITH FROG AND TOAD"
by Theatr Iolo, Kevin Lewis & Sarah Blackburn,
Photography Terry Morgan

Lurking Truth / Gwir sy'n Llechu

Gwynfryn, Newtown Rd, Machynlleth, Powys SY20 8EY

Tel/Ffôn **+44 (0) 1654 702200**
Email/Ebost **davidian@rabey.fsbusiness.co.uk**

Artistic Director/Cyfarwyddwr Artistig: **David Ian Rabey**
Administrator/Gweinyddydd: **David Ian Rabey**

Artistic Policy Polisi Artistig:

To arrest, fascinate and seduce audiences beyond the current fear of art which is not defined by tourism and utilitarian community celebration (of what, for whom, at whose behest?).

To demonstrate the self-renewing immediacy of theatrical performance in which language is a promise written in the air and physicality is the ballet of manifested courage.

To achieve a production style that is appropriate to the uniqueness of the play rather than to the reassuring familiarities of theatrical convention.

To show how complexity can, in theatre as in other matters, actually be more enjoyable and exciting than predictability, and how theatre can be a living triumph of the artificial, which is what human beings do best.

To present new work written by the Artistic Director or exhilarating re-evaluations of major works by modern dramatists neglected in a climate of theatrical cowardice.

Past Productions Cynhyrchiadau'r Gorffennol:

Victory; Don't Exaggerate; The Castle (1986); The Bewitched; No Truth on the Cheap (1987); The Back of Beyond; The Back of Beyond (Back with a Vengeance ReMix) (1996); AC/DC; Bite or Suck (1997); The Battle of the Crows (1998); The Twelfth Battle of Isonzo (2001).

Future Plans Cynlluniau at y dyfodol:

In 2002, Lurking Truth plans wider performances of 'The Twelfth Battle of Isonzo', the English-language premiere of a new text written and directed by Howard Barker. This is a co-production with the Irish theatre company Íomhá Ildánach, supported by the British Council and the Irish Arts Council, which was acclaimed as 'an important event in Irish theatre' when it opened in Dublin Project in Summer 2001.

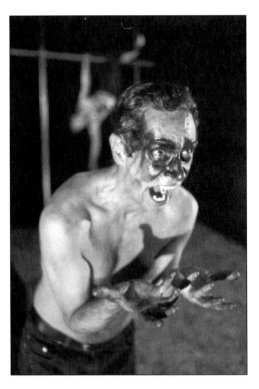

"BITE OR SUCK" Photography Keith Morris

Man Troi

Rose Haven, Allt Fach, Llandudoch,
Pembrokeshire SA43 3HA

Tel/*Ffôn*	**+44 (0) 1239 613148**
Tel/*Ffôn*	**+44 (0) 7813 199 136** (mobile)
Fax/*Ffacs*	**+44 (0) 1239 613148**
Email/*Ebost*	**joshapland@yahoo.co.uk**
Web/*Y Wê*	**To be opened in 2002**

Artistic Director/*Cyfarwyddwr Artistig*: **Jo Shapland**
Administrator/*Gweinyddydd*: **Joanna Roberts**
Technical Contact /*Cyswllt Technegol*: **Joanna Roberts**

Artistic Policy Polisi Artistig:

To continuously produce challenging and experimental work - incorporating live physical performance and the sonic and visual arts. We are looking to work site-specifically and not to be theatre constrained.

Company History Hanes y Cwmni:

Originated from Jo Shapland's solo dance / performance work which often involved collaboration with other artists of varying disciplines and abilities. Man Troi established in 2001.

Past Productions Cynhyrchiadau'r Gorffennol:

Chrysalis (1996-98)**; Zeitlupe** (1999)**; Pedestal** (2001-02)**; Soluna** (2001)**; See the Woods through the Trees** (2001)**.**

Future Plans Cynlluniau at y dyfodol:

Exhibition of Soluna Project (incorporating Pedestal, See the Woods and Soluna) will take place at Chapter Arts Centre, Cardiff in March 2002. Site-specific Pedestal residencies in Europe being planned from 2002 onwards. Collaboration between Jo Shapland and director Phillip Zarrilli in 2002.

Music Theatre Wales

Perch Buildings, 20 West Bute St,
Cardiff CF10 5EP

Tel/*Ffôn* **+44 (0) 29 2049 8471**
Fax/*Ffacs* **+44 (0) 29 2049 8472**
Email/*Ebost* **enquiries@musictheatrewales.org.uk**
Web/*Y Wê* **www.musictheatrewales.org.uk**

Artistic Directors/*Cyfarwyddwyr Artistig:* **Michael McCarthy**, Artistic Director
Michael Rafferty, Music Director

Administrator/*Gweinyddwyr:* **Abigail Pogson**
General Manager/*Rheolwraig Gyffredinol*
Nick Allsop, Production Manager

Artistic Policy Polisi Artistig:
Touring contemporary chamber opera through Wales, England and beyond.

Company History Hanes y Cwmni:
Established in 1988, MTW exists to perform contemporary classics and commissioned works through the UK. It has created 16 new productions, of which five have been commissioned pieces.

It is regularly asked to perform its work abroad.

Its performances are accompanied and supported by education and outreach events.

Past Productions Cynhyrchiadau'r Gorffennol:
Punch and Judy; The Rape of Lucia; Jane Eyre; The Lighthouse.

Future Plans Cynlluniau at y dyfodol:
Gwynneth and the Green Knight; The Electrification of the Soviet Union (2002)**; Ion** (2003)**.**

"JANE EYRE" Photography Dave Daggers

Theatr na n'Óg

Uned 3, Ystad Ddiwydiannol Heol Millands,
Castell Nedd SA11 1NJ

Tel/*Ffôn*	**+44 (0) 1639 641771**
Fax/*Ffacs*	**+44 (0) 1639 647941**
Email/*Ebost*	**cwmni@theatr-nanog.co.uk**
Web/*Y Wê*	**www.theatr-nanog.co.uk**

Artistic Director/*Cyfarwyddwr Artistig:* **Geinor Jones**
Administrator/*Gweinyddydd:* **Janet Huxtable**

Artistic Policy Polisi Artistig:

The company creates productions and projects in Welsh and English that entertain and educate children and young people of all ages, enhancing and encouraging their perception of theatre as a vibrant medium.

The company seeks at all times and in all respects to produce theatre of the highest quality, that is seen by audiences within and beyond its region.

Company History Hanes y Cwmni:

Fifteen years after its establishment, the innovative Neath based professional theatre company has changed its name from Theatre West Glamorgan to Theatr na n'Óg - literally meaning 'theatre of the eternal young'.

Past Productions Cynhyrchiadau'r Gorffennol:

Cider with Rosie; Jac Tar; Brodyr y Garreg Ddu / Brother and Black Diamonds; Spam Man; A Child's Christmas in Wales.

Future Plans Cynlluniau at y dyfodol:

To continue to work locally, nationally and internationally providing theatre of the highest standard to people of all ages. Develop partnerships and close relationships with numerous theatres, enhancing our artistic programme and offering diverse theatrical provision to our audiences.

Nofit State Circus

PO Box 238, Cardiff CF24 0XS

Tel/Ffôn   **+44 (0) 29 2048 8734**
Fax/Ffacs   **+44 (0) 29 2041 0547** phone tel number first!
Email/Ebost   **info@nofitstate.com**
Web/Y Wê   **www.nofitstatecircus.co.uk**
            www.nofitstate.com

Artistic Directors/Cyfarwyddwyr Artistig: **Ali Williams, Tom Rack, Orit Azaz**
Administrator/Gweinyddydd: **Tim Adam**

Artistic Policy Polisi Artistig:

To produce through collaboration with experts from other fields, progressive and excellent mixed media circus, both with professional artists and through community projects, accessible to the wider community throughout Wales, the UK and beyond. The company has a 350 seater Big Top and a 1000 capacity Unique Silver Spaceship tent!

Company History Hanes y Cwmni:

Founded in 1985, the company has developed from performing street and cabaret shows into the UK's leading contemporary touring circus.

The ACW, CCC and private sponsorship have funded the company's work. The company is well know in Wales for large scale mixed media community projects involving up to 250 performers, and for professional touring shows.

More recently ACW lottery has funded 'The Stepping Stones' project (full history on the web site).

Past Productions Cynhyrchiadau'r Gorffennol:

All productions are company devised with writers being involved in the later stages. **Alice; Treasure Island; Faust; Now-here; Prophecy.**

Future Plans Cynlluniau at y dyfodol:

To produce three large-scale community projects in Wales that evolve into large professional touring products. These will use circus, dance, music and technology in the new spectacular tented structure.

Pearson / Brookes

'Bodwenog', Llangranog, Llandysul,
Ceredigion SA44 6SQ

Tel/Ffôn   **+44 (0) 1239 654136**
Email/Ebost   **mip@aber.ac.uk**
         mail@mikebrookes.com
Web/Y Wê   **www.mikebrookes.com/ambivalence/**
         pearsonbrookes/default.htm

Artistic Directors/*Cyfarwyddwyr Artistig:* **Mike Brookes/Mike Pearson**

Artistic Policy Polisi Artistig:

Pearson/Brookes represents the recent and on-going collaboration between Mike Brookes and Mike Pearson, their collective proposals and theories, and the performance works they produce. As individuals their work has encompassed and engaged an array of media and disciplines, within the development of an innovative artistic and performance practice spanning decades. They met in Cardiff, and first worked together, on Brith Gof's 'Gododdin' in 1988.

Pearson/Brookes is dedicated to the pursuit of experimental strategies and practice in the form, function and placement of performance; an attempt to bring contemporary sensibilities and technologies to the past as a form of cultural stimulation which values memory, opinion, speculation, and to create work that is both conceptual and discursive.

Mike Pearson and Mike Brookes are currently developing forms of participatory performance, responsive to changed political circumstances; forms that problematise notions of 'character' and 'plot', the means by which dramatic material is generated and exhibited, and pose important questions about the nature of theatrical representation. Their practice constitutes performance as social enquiry and action rather than simple artistic reflection.

Past Productions Cynhyrchiadau'r Gorffennol:

Dead Men's shoes (1997)**; The first five miles, Body of evidence, The man who ate his boots** (1998)**; Just a bit of history repeating,** (work in progress) (1999)**; Like a pelican in the wilderness (towards the north: act 1)** (2000).

"THE MAN WHO ATE HIS BOOTS"
Photography Keith Morris

Theatr Powys

The Drama Centre, Tremont Rd, Llandrindod, Powys LD1 5EB

Tel/Ffón   **+44 (0) 1597 824444**
Fax/Ffacs   **+44 (0) 1597 824381**
Email/Ebost   **theatr.powys@powys.gov.uk**
Web/Y Wê   **www.theatrpowys.co.uk**

Artistic Director/Cyfarwyddwr Artistig: **Ian Yeoman**
Administrator/Gweinyddydd: **Nikki Leopold**

Artistic Policy Polisi Artistig:

Theatr Powys is an exciting and innovative Company, devising and creating original, participatory theatre-in-education programmes for students of all ages in Powys schools. The Company also undertakes a programme of Community Touring Theatre to young people and their families in village halls, community centres, arts centres and theatres across Powys and wider Wales. Theatr Powys is committed to young people; their experiences, problems and engagement with the world. The condition of the young, and the role of the imagination in the free development of young people, is central to the artistic and educational agenda of the Company. Further to our touring work we are proud to manage the award winning Mid Powys Youth Theatre.

Company History Hanes y Cwmni:

For almost 30 years Theatr Powys has lived in mid Wales developing close and lasting relationships with schools, community groups and individuals in pursuit of work that can truly be called a community provision. One of the original network of eight Welsh young people's and community Companies, we continue to receive support from Powys County Council and the Arts Council of Wales. Numerous theatre artists have worked with us and return to work again. The Company has contributed significantly to the development of new writing in Wales and the youth theatre provision has offered a secure grounding for young people who have chosen to continue their training in the theatre arts.

The Company remains committed to the methodology and practice of TIE and the production of new plays that build a broad community audience of young and old alike. The Company also contributes significantly to the developing of International links and was proud to be associated with the 'People in Movement' International Conference in Amman, Jordan in August 2000.

Past Productions Cynhyrchiadau'r Gorffennol:

Morgiana's Dance; The Little Clay People; Y Bobl Bach Clai; Wind; Safa'n Saff (1999)**; Minimata; Pillow of Glass; Fi fy hun; A Comedy of Errors; Cinderella** (2000)**; The Apothecary's Story; Chance Children; Plant Ffawd; Antigone; Fuente Ovejuna; Christmas Carol** (2001)**.**

Future Plans Cynlluniau at y dyfodol:

The Company seeks to contribute to the ongoing development of arts provision strategies for young people in Wales.

Photography Keith Morris

Red Button

3 Thomas St, Penygraig, Rhondda CF40 1EU

Artistic Directors/*Cyfarwyddwyr Artistig*: **Dixie Dickenson**
Dafydd Williams

Administrators/*Gweinyddwyr*: **Dixie Dickenson**
Dafydd Williams

Artistic Policy Polisi Artistig:

Committed to the performance of new writing in Wales.
To tour relevant accessible people's theatre.

Company History Hanes y Cwmni:

Previously a co-operative.
Became a limited company in 2000.
Performances at Dempsey's pub theatre, Trelewis Community Centre and the Swansea Grand Theatre.

Past Productions Cynhyrchiadau'r Gorffennol:

Scorched Earth; Building of Venice; Precious.

Future Plans Cynlluniau at y dyfodol:

To further work by Alan Osborne;
to secure funding;
to take a production to the Edinburgh fringe;
to prove the Welsh establishment is wrong.

Sean Tuan John

15, Denton Rd, Canton, Cardiff CF5 1PD

Tel/*Ffôn* **+44 (0) 7712 208998**

Artistic Director/*Cyfarwyddwr Artistig*: **Sean Tuan John**

Artistic Policy Polisi Artistig:

A kind of theatre that draws on kitsch elements, as well as poetic realism.

Company History Hanes y Cwmni:

Sean Tuan John is a young choreographer, based in South Wales, gaining an international reputation for work that is exciting, innovative and articulate. The physical language of the productions is tough, dynamic and quirky. The unusual use of fast floor sequences and a gestural language is both refined and poetic. The work has toured nationally and internationally to venues and festivals in Belgium, Austria, Holland, Germany and France.

Past Productions Cynhyrchiadau'r Gorffennol:

Frederick's First Kiss; The Boy who never came back; Hanging Out With Jesus; Poor White Trash; Dances for Aliens (with Bert van Gorp); **O Brutus.**

"DANCES WITH ALIENS"
Photography Jos Verhoogen

Sgript Cymru, Contemporary Drama Wales

Chapter, Market Rd, Canton, Cardiff CF5 1QE

Tel/*Ffôn*   **+44 (0) 29 2023 6650**
Fax/*Ffacs*   **+44 (0) 29 2023 6651**
Email/*Ebost*   **sgriptcymru@sgriptcymru.com**

Artistic Director/*Cyfarwyddwr Artistig*: **Simon Harris**
Artistic Associate/*Cyswllt Artistig*: **Bethan Jones**
Literary Manager/*Rheolwr Llenyddol*: **Bill Hopkinson**
Administrative Director/*Cyfarwyddwr Gweinyddol*: **Mai Jones**

Artistic Policy Polisi Artistig:

The mission of the company is to discover, develop and produce the best work of contemporary Welsh and Wales-based playwrights.

Prif amcanion y cwmni yw darganfod, datblygu a chynhyrchu y gwaith gorau gan awduron cyfoes Cymru.

Company History Hanes y Cwmni:

Formed in May 2000, Sgript Cymru evolved out of the successful Welsh language company, Dalier Sylw, led by Artistic Director, Bethan Jones, which enjoyed 10 years championing a fresh generation of Welsh language playwrights to audiences throughout Wales. As part of its core activity, Sgript Cymru offers a reading service, commissions new plays in Welsh and English, regularly hosts a development forum for new work called Sgript Xplosure! and presents its own productions, such as *Art and Guff* by Catherine Tregenna, as well as working in co-production with companies such as Paines Plough on *Crazy Gary's Mobile Disco* by Gary Owen, and Theatr Gwynedd on Meic Povey's double bill *Diwedd y Byd / Yr Hen Blant*.

Fe ffurfiwyd Sgript Cymru ym Mai 2000, ac mae wedi esblygu o'r cwmni ysgrifennu newydd llwyddiannus, Dalier Sylw, a fu'n datblygu cenhedlaeth ffres o awduron ar gyfer cynulleidfaoedd led led Cymru am ddegawd, dan arweinyddiaeth y Cyfarwyddwr Artistig, Bethan Jones. Fel rhan o'r gweithgaredd craidd, mae Sgript Cymru yn cynnig gwasanaeth darllen, yn comisiynu gwaith newydd yn Gymraeg a Saesneg, yn cynnal eu fforwn datblygu gwaith newydd rheolaidd, Sgipt Xplosure!, ac yn cynhyrchu dramau megis **Art and Guff** *gan Catherine Tregenna, yn ogystal â chydweithio gyda chwmniau megis Paines Plough ar* **Crazy Gary's Mobile Disco** *gan Gary Owen a Theatr Gwynedd ar* **Diwedd y Byd / Yr Hen Blant** *gan Meic Povey.*

Past Productions Cynhyrchiadau'r Gorffennol:

Diwedd y Byd/Yr Hen Blant; Art and Guff; Crazy Gary's Mobile Disco; Ysbryd Beca; Mab.

Future Plans Cynlluniau at y dyfodol:

Building on its first year's work, the company will continue to nurture and produce the best theatre writing that Wales can offer. Productions for 2002 include *Franko's Bastard* by Dic Edwards, *Dosbarth Digrifwch* by Geraint Lewis and *Past Away* by Tracy Harris. Other activities will include the development of a Young Writers Group and creation of a Wales-wide network of development activity through its Community Writer Initiative.

Wrth adeiladu ar waith y flwyddyn gyntaf, bydd y cwmni yn parhau i feithrin a chynhyrchu y gwaith gorau y gall Cymru ei gynnig. Yn ystod 2002, bwriedir cynhyrchu **Franko's Bastard** *gan Dic Edwards,* **Dosbarth Digrifwch** *gan Geraint Lewis a* **Past Away** *gan Tracy Harris. Bydd gweithgareddau eraill yn cynnys datblygiad Grwp Ysgrifenwyr Ifanc, a chreu rhwydwaith cenedlaethol o weithgaredd trwy eu cynllun Awduron Bro.*

"CRAZY GARY'S MOBILE DISCO" by Gary Owen Photography Manuel Harlan

Sherman Theatre Ltd

Senghennydd Rd, Cardiff CF24 4YE

Tel/*Ffôn*   **+44 (0) 29 2064 6901** admin
            +44 (0) 29 2064 6900 box office
            +44 (0) 29 2064 6909 minicom
Fax/*Ffacs*   **+44 (0) 29 2064 6902**
Email/*Ebost* **admin@shermantheatre.demon.co.uk**
Artistic Director/*Cyfarwyddwr Artistig:* **Phil Clark**
Administrator/*Gweinyddydd:* **Margaret Jones**
            General Manager/*Rheolwraig Gyffredinol*

Artistic Policy Polisi Artistig:

The Sherman is one of Britain's premier theatres for young people and is the major producing and presenting venue in South Wales.

Our mission is to create a fresh, exciting, invigorating and immediate theatre experience in an open and vital environment for young people, who are at the heart of our policy.

We are committed to raising the status of theatre on the leisure agenda of young people; we aim to realise this by presenting a wide range of British and International, high quality theatre alongside Sherman Theatre Company productions at home and abroad; we celebrate our youth theatre and education activities and the work of our visiting companies.

We aim to promote this unique spirit and style of theatre which will enrich the experience of all our audiences, regardless of age, our amateur and community participants and our youth theatre members.

Company History Hanes y Cwmni:

For the past 10 years, the Sherman Theatre has been at the forefront of presenting diverse and distinctive theatre for the young people of South Wales and beyond. Our resident professional Sherman Theatre Company ensures that our work is relevant, exciting and at the forefront of the arts in Wales and the UK with shows on tour throughout the country, representing Wales on a national stage. And each week our eleven Sherman Youth theatre groups provide an opportunity for over 200 young people to participate in and create their own theatre.

Past Productions Cynhyrchiadau'r Gorffennol:

The Jungle Book; All's Fair; POP; Horrible Histories - Crackers Christmas; Puff The Magic Dragon; Big Brother is watching you; Saturday Night Forever; The Enormous Crocodile, James and the Giant Peach (2000-01).

Future Plans Cynlluniau at y dyfodol:

Return of BBC Radio Wales lunchtime play series April 2002. Development of Venue 3 as a venue for rehearsed readings and new performance. co-productions with Welsh College of Music and Drama (WCMD) and a partner in the Cardiff International Festival of Musical Theatre autumn 2002. Plus full seasons of Sherman Theatre Company work.

Simon Whitehead

Penrhiw, Abercych, Pembrokeshire SA37 0HB

Tel/Ffôn   **+44 (0) 1239 841488**
Fax/Ffacs   **+44 (0) 1239 841488**

Email/Ebost   **white.simon@virgin.net**
Web/Y Wê   **www.untitledstates.net**

Artistic Director/Cyfarwyddwr Artistig: **Simon Whitehead**

Artistic Policy Polisi Artistig:

To make live, ephemeral performance works that aim to reveal the shifting landscape of relationships to place, territory and belonging in an age of increasing mobility and change.

Company History Hanes y Cwmni:

Movement Artist Simon Whitehead began making work in 1992 as part of the live art collective 'The Working Party', in London. During this period he made a series of walking and interventionist works in public spaces and the studio works 'The Assignment Series', presented at the Serpentine Gallery, ICA and Chisenhale Dance Space. Following a period of further movement training and performances in New York he returned to Wales in 1994, where he developed the performance work 'Bodies of Land' in the Preseli Hills with Scott deLahunta, and toured the solo work 'shed (from walking)'. Since 1996 he has developed a collaborative relationship with sound artist Barnaby Oliver through a body of performance works that incorporate an attitude to making that is bound by underlying notions of deep ecology, presence and an intuitive approach to site. Their research process is place-sensitive and often involves periods of walking and the gathering of materials from which to ritually reconstruct a 'magical model' of a landscape, in these live movement /sound works the presence/interaction of the viewer is an essential component (see past productions). In 1999 Simon collaborated with film director Margaret Constantas on 'Anemos', a short dance film for BBC Wales made on a windfarm site. In the Autumn 2000, he collaborated with Performance Artist Rachel Rosenthal on a journey from the source to the estuary of the river Ystwyth; 'The Rivers Journey' was curated by CPR. In July 2000 Whitehead and Oliver were commissioned to make the durational sound/performance work somasonicspirit for the between nature ecology/performance symposium at Lancaster University, presented later that summer in Cardiff in association with Chapter. Simon was a contributing artist on the WRA / La Caldera 'Migrations' conference at the CCCB Barcelona, where he developed 'stalks' a work in response to the city and some of its animal inhabitants. 'stalks' was developed further in Cardiff in 2001, when Whitehead followed four men on their journeys across the city; this work commissioned by Chapter Arts Centre was presented as a four monitor video piece and now exists in a CDRom version (designed by Barnaby Oliver). In 2001 Whitehead initiated the project 'ointment', a live art event in farm outbuildings involving seven artists from West Wales and beyond. He produced the short video work 'wooden horse' in April 2001, in response to the proposed GM tests near his home in Pembrokeshire, recently shown at gallery 39 in Cardiff. 'Haunts', a project initiated at Chisenhale Dance Space London, began with Whitehead working with 7-10 year old children, generating performance from their experiences of walking to and from school. This project was then developed in a rural community in Wicklow, Ireland, with children and elderly people making invited interventions into a live sound installation. Whitehead was invited to be artist in residence at the Boreal Art/Nature centre in Quebec, Canada in

September, where he followed a period of research leading to a short performance work in a forest, 'vein'. Since 1995 he has continued to develop the 'locator series', workshop residencies for movement and performance artists, exploring the ground between ecology and performance; locator#10 took place with 10 artists over 10 days in October in Tycanol woods West Wales. This research is ongoing.

Past Productions Cynhyrchiadau'r Gorffennol:

locator series (1995); **big muff** (1996); **salt/halen** (1996-97); **folcland** (1997); **tableland 1,11 &111** (1998-99); **skyclad; Anemos** (1999)**; testing; somasonicspirit; somasonics; rivers journey; stalks** (2000); **stalks (Cardiff); butterfly in the sun; nightrider (ointment); wooden horse; haunts; vein (Quebec)** (2001).

Future Plans Cynlluniau at y dyfodol:

homing; development project; itinerancy and perception in performance, video, sound. Preview at G39 / Chapter Cardiff, April 2002 (see website); **2 miles an hour;** work made on a walk from Wales to London, with visual artist Pete Bodenham. Sept 2002. **travelling without moving;** research into telematics, sound and movement, for installation in a public space. To be realised 2003. **ointment;** group show/live art in situ/West Wales. Summer 2002. **locator;** continued research in Tycanol West Wales and in Nottingham with Dance4 in summer 2002, with planned publication.

Slush

7 Cliff Terrace, Aberystwyth
Ceredigion SY23 2DN

Tel/*Ffôn*   +44 (0) 7773 795689
             +44 (0) 7866 552277

Email/*Ebost*   andy@slushtheatre.co.uk
                gary@slushtheatre.co.uk
                naomi@slushtheatre.co.uk
                rob@slushtheatre.co.uk

Web/*Y Wê*   www.slushtheatre.co.uk

Artistic Directors/*Cyfarwyddwyr Artistig*: **Gary Owen**
                                            Andy Cornforth
                                            Naomi Jalil
                                            Rob Storr

Artistic Policy Polisi Artistig:

Slush are engaged in empirical research into the nature of STORY.

Past Productions Cynhyrchiadau'r Gorffennol:

Hated Nightfall (1998) **Fags** (2002)**.**

Future Plans Cynlluniau at y dyfodol:

In autumn 2002 Slush will premiere 'Shhh, A Quiet Night in with Naomi Jalil'. Written by Alexandra Bendelow it will tour throughout Wales and the rest of the UK in 2003. They will then premiere a new play by Gary Owen in autumn 2003.

Small World Theatre

Fern Villa, Llandygwydd, Cardigan SA43 2QX

Tel/*Ffôn*   **+44 (0) 1239 682785**
Fax/*Ffacs*   **+44 (0) 1239 682785**
Email/*Ebost*   **smallworld@enterprise.net**
Web/*Y Wê*   **www.smallworld.org.uk**

Artistic Directors/*Cyfarwyddwyr Artistig*: **Bill Hamblett, Ann Shrosbree**
Administrator/*Gweinyddydd*: **David Gillam**

Artistic Policy Polisi Artistig:

To use the universal language of theatre to communicate important ideas and feelings to young people and adults in a non-exploitative way.
To experiment with techniques which increase the effectiveness and excitement of live performance.
To promote international cultural links through theatre.
To learn from other cultures.
To write produce and perform shows that reflect local and global concerns that are common to all people.
To teach and exchange skills with interested groups including extensionists, teachers, artists and other performers.
To increase the status of puppetry within theatre, film and TV as well as with public and private funders and sponsors.

Company History Hanes y Cwmni:

Small World Theatre produces original performances for theatres, and new audiences in unusual venues, which challenge the distinction between actors and animates. The company also implements projects using the arts in development and provides consultants to bodies such as the UN, British Council and INGO's. Founder members Ann Shrosbree and Bill Hamblett, who have worked together since 1979, have experience of working with poor or marginalised communities in Vietnam, Nepal, India, Zambia, Sudan, Kenya, Tanzania, Wales, Ireland and in Inner City areas of the UK. They continue to design and implement development awareness projects in the UK and produce innovative performances using theatre, puppetry, storytelling and new technology. They provide training and workshops that often lead to performances with community groups, as well as events such as street processions with giant puppets and other site specific events.

SWT's international work in culture for development, participatory theatre, rights and democracy, informs and is informed by touring performances in theatres for Welsh and other UK audiences.

SWT occupies a unique position in Welsh theatre culture.

Past Productions Cynhyrchiadau'r Gorffennol:

Shades of Celtic Folk (1991); **In the Shadow of the City** (1990/2); **Padlock Jones; Manifiesto de la Selva** (1992); **Moving!** (1993); **Touring Moving!** (1994/7); **Captain Slaughterboard Drops Anchor; First stage production** (1995); **Angorfa Capten Lladdfwrdd** (1996); performances for **Streets of the South;** Giant Street Puppets for **Clonmel; Manifiesto de la Selva 2** (1997/8); **File not Found** (1998); **Mufaro** (1999); **Generation X** (2000); **Beats the box; DIOGEL?/SAFE?** (2001); See web site for details of other performance activities.

Spectacle Theatre

Pontypridd College, Rhondda Campus,
Llwynypia, Tonypandy CF40 2TQ

Tel/Ffôn	**+44 (0) 1443 430700**
Fax/Ffacs	**+44 (0) 1443 423080**
Email/Ebost	**info@spectacletheatre.co.uk**
Web/Y Wê	**www.spectacletheatre.co.uk**

Artistic Director/Cyfarwyddwr Artistig: **Steve Davis**
Administrator/Gweinyddydd: **Sandra Jones**

Artistic Policy Polisi Artistig:

Spectacle Theatre Company is committed to producing innovative and accessible theatre for, and with, theatres and Community / Youth Centres.

We provide Theatre in Education and a specialised Theatre for Young People programme for schools and Further Education establishments throughout South Wales.

Spectacle develops new writing through the commissioning of scripts and Company devised work in both Welsh and English.

Our aim is to make the Arts inclusive and accessible to all members of our community.

Company History Hanes y Cwmni:

Formed in 1979, Spectacle is the Community Theatre Company for the Glamorgan Valleys. Based in the Rhondda, Spectacle has an international reputation for excellence, innovation and collaboration.

We provide a comprehensive service including performances, workshops and Inset training for teachers. By working closely with subject advisors and teachers, we ensure our work is both relevant and stimulating.Our follow-up materials are used to enrich the performance and extend the learning experience.

Spectacle Theatre's role is to include members of our community in the experience of live Theatre, as spectator or participant. We aim to provide these people with a unique experience through working alongside the professional artist.

In 1998, Spectacle became the first professional Theatre Company to win an Investors in People Award and remains committed to training its staff to achieve its primary objective - to create a rewarding artistic, educational and social opportunity through performance and workshops.

Past Productions Cynhyrchiadau'r Gorffennol:

Cam Gwag; Delwedd; Moon River; The Deal (1993)**; My Name Is Me; Breaking The Ice; Shakespeare Factory** (1994)**; Sending Signals; Order and Disorder; The Man Who Gave His Foot For Love** (1995)**; David; Un Nos Ar Faes Peryddon** (1996)**; Vertigo; Kid** (1997)**; Pop; Wedi'r Haf; Freewheelers** (1998)**; Over Milk Wood; House; Bag Dancing; Rhiwgarn Underground; Through The Cat Flap** (1999)**; Welsh Anthem; Find Me; Antigone Now!; Kid; Guto; Balance** (2000)**; Bystanders/Y Gwylwyr; The Lazy Ant; Hide & Seek/Chwarae Cuddio; Glyncornel** - Youth Theatre (2001)**.

Future Plans Cynlluniau at y dyfodol:

The Brundibar Project; Into the East; Daring to Speak (2002)**.

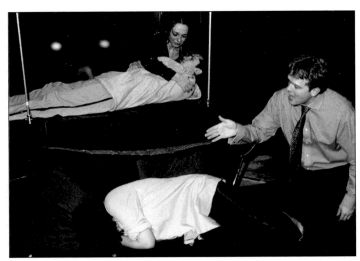

Photography Terry Morgan

Steel Wasp Theatre Co

c/o Taliesin Arts Centre, University of Wales
Swansea, Singleton Park, Swansea

Tel/Ffôn   **+44 (0) 7968 480703**
Email/Ebost   **nickywasp@hotmail.com**

Artistic Directors/*Cyfarwyddwyr Artistig:* **Nick Evans, Alison O'Connor**

Artistic Policy Polisi Artistig:

Steel Wasp work from their Swansea base to create and tour new Welsh work and quality productions of existing texts. Their work is highly visual and fuses drama, physicality and music. The company has a highly successful policy of outreach work, with schools, colleges and community groups across Wales. Theatre for and about Wales, performed by a company from Wales.

Company History Hanes y Cwmni:

The company formed in 1997 when a group of graduates returned from across the border with the intent of creating a new theatre company in the Swansea area. Their 4 year history has seen them perform in venues as diverse as The Sherman, Ystradgynlais Welfare Hall and Bristol Old Vic, and the company has also undertaken international work in Sweden and Prague. They have also developed a strong workshop programme across a series of institutions in South Wales. The projects undertaken so far have included new writing, devising, classics and established Welsh writing. They retain a strong commitment to, where possible, working with Welsh-based actors, as well as providing opportunities for Welsh exiles to return and enrich the South West Wales artistic community.

Past Productions Cynhyrchiadau'r Gorffennol:

East From the Gantry (1997)**; Garageland; Rising Tide** (1999)**; The Suicide; East From the Gantry** (2000)**.**

Future Plans Cynlluniau at y dyfodol:

The company will continue to tour existing productions in rep, and will stage a new production in the year 2001. The company is interested in developing its hitherto successful international policy and is looking to find international venues and festivals which may be interested in its work.

"EAST FROM THE GANTRY"

Swansea Ballet Russe

Fern Villa, Llandygwydd, Cardigan SA43 2QX

Tel/*Ffôn*	**+44 (0) 1792 455833**
	+44 (0) 7733 488 369 technical/*technegol*
	+44 (0) 7887 943 577 ballet/*bale*
	+44 (0) 1792 475242 marketing/*marchnata*
Fax/*Ffacs*	**+44 (0) 1792 475379**
Email/*Ebost*	**paul.hopkins2@swansea.gov.uk**
Web/*Y Wê*	**www.smallworld.org.uk**

Technical/*Technegol*: **Mikhail Vorona**
Ballet/*Bale*: **Chika Temma**
Marketing/*Marchnata*: **Paul Hopkins**

Artistic Policy Polisi Artistig:

Since making Swansea Grand Theatre their permanent home in 1999, the dancers have dedicated themselves to taking their art form to communities and venues across Britain that would normally be excluded from such professional tours.

Company History Hanes y Cwmni:

Ballet Russe is a group of young dancers all trained in the classical Russian style of Ballet. The dancers have appeared at many theatres all over the world, performing classical and modern Russian Ballet repertoires (Giselle, Les Sylphides, Swan Lake, etc. All of the dancers are graduates from the Vaganova Ballet School or the Moscow Academy of Ballet.

Past Productions Cynhyrchiadau'r Gorffennol:

Giselle; Les Sylphides; Paquita; Romeo & Juliet; Coppelia; The Nutcracker (Suite and full length)**; Gala Programmes featuring Don Quixote, Tarantella, Sleeping Beauty and more.**

Future Plans Cynlluniau at y dyfodol:

La fille mal gardee (2002).

Thin Language Theatre Company

c/o Sgript Cymru, Contemporary Drama Wales Chapter, Market Rd, Canton, Cardiff CF5 1QE

Tel/Ffôn   **+44 (0) 29 2023 6650**
Fax/Ffacs   **+44 (0) 29 2023 6651**
Email/Ebost   **sgriptcymru@sgriptcymru.com**

Artistic Policy Polisi Artistig:

"The English language is a thin language", is a saying in Welsh.

Thin Language Theatre Company was established in 1992 by Simon Harris, Natasha Betteridge and Michael Sheen. The aim was to create dynamic and distinctive theatre in English that reflected the richness of contemporary Wales through new work: new plays, revivals, adaptations and translations. Allied to our experience as Anglo-Welsh, the company aims to contribute to a richer language of Welsh theatre in English.

Company History Hanes y Cwmni:

Established in 1992 by Simon Harris with Natasha Betteridge and Michael Sheen, the company was launched with a reading at the Sherman Theatre of an adaptation of Caradoc Evans' novel 'Nothing to Pay'. In the autumn of 1993, the company produced a Welsh-inflected version of the Quebecois playwright Michel Tremblay's 'Forever Yours Marie Lou'. The version was written by Sian Evans and explored themes of identity, belonging and renewal on a personal and metaphorical level, implicitly drawing comparisons between the bilingual cultures of Wales and Quebec. The Times commended "the cracking ensemble playing" and "an engrossing performance".

Past Productions Cynhyrchiadau'r Gorffennol:

Forever Yours Marie Lou; Nothing To Pay; Badfinger.

Future Plans Cynlluniau at y dyfodol:

The company has no plans to produce work in the near future. Simon Harris is a playwright and Associate Director of Sgript Cymru, Natasha Betteridge is Artistic Director of Northampton Theatres and Michael Sheen is pursuing his acting career.

The Torch Theatre

St Peter's Rd, Milford Haven,
Pembrokeshire SA73 2BU

Tel/*Ffôn*	**+44 (0) 1646 695267** box office
	+44 (0) 1646 694192 admin
Fax/*Ffacs*	**+44 (0) 1646 698919**
	+44 (0) 1646 693605 marketing/tech
Email/*Ebost*	**info@torchtheatre.co.uk**
Web/*Y Wê*	**www.torchtheatre.co.uk**

Artistic Director/*Cyfarwyddwr Artistig*: **Peter Doran**
Finance Director/*Cyfarwyddwr Cyllid*: **Roland Williams**
Marketing & Administrative Officer/*Swyddog Marchnata a Gweinyddu*: **Jane Evans**
Head of Lighting and Sound/*Pennaeth Goleuo a Sain*: **David Goffin**

Artistic Policy Polisi Artistig:

The Torch Theatre exists to produce quality theatre for Milford Haven and the surrounding areas. Its aims and objectives are to provide a mix of live theatre events that audiences find distinctive, accessible, often challenging and which stimulate interest and deepen engagement with the performing arts. It also aims to provide outreach work for schools and communities in the form of workshops, talks, seminars and other work related to the theatre programme.

Company History Hanes y Cwmni:

Since November 1977, when The Torch Theatre opened, The Torch Theatre Company has involved itself with the community, been part of the community and has created an increasing interest in, and awareness of, the arts in an area which hitherto had no tradition of professional theatre.

Past Productions Cynhyrchiadau'r Gorffennol:

Godspell (1980)**; Playboy of the Western World** (1988)**; Under Milk Wood** (1990)**; The Woman in Black** (1998)**; Abigail's Party** (1999)**; Blue Remembered Hills; Little Shop of Horrors** (2000)**.**

Future Plans Cynlluniau at y dyfodol:

Over the next 3 years The Torch Theatre will aim to take more positive steps to revitalise its programme and broaden and substantially increase its audience. This will be achieved by aggressive and positive marketing. Our vision is for The Torch to be viewed as the centre for arts in Pembrokeshire.

Touched Theatre

23 Kerrycroy St, Cardiff CF24 2AQ

Tel/*Ffôn*	**+44 (0) 7764 193696**
Email/*Ebost*	**s.marmion@theatreroyal.com**
Web/*Y Wê*	**freespace.virgin.net/steve.marmion**

Artistic Director/*Cyfarwyddwr Artistig*: **Steve Marmion**

Artistic Policy Polisi Artistig:

We aim to produce live and dynamic performances for theatre's old and new audiences.

We are a stepping stone company for graduates and young performers to move from training into the industry. Our work ranges from new writing to classic adaptations.

It is always new work.

Company History Hanes y Cwmni:

The company was founded in 1996 by Daniel Brown, Jon Lee, Steve Marmion, Andrew Morrison and Adam Rush - Graduates of the Theatre and Media Drama BA awarded by the University of Glamorgan and the Welsh College of Music and Drama. The company has achieved repeated critical acclaim from audiences and the press.

Past Productions Cynhyrchiadau'r Gorffennol:

97 (1996); **Caliban's Island; Sleep** (1997); **The Club; Desiderata** (1998); **Rhino** (1999); **The Visit** (2000).

Future Plans Cynlluniau at y dyfodol:

We intend to produce a piece for the Edinburgh Festival in the foreseeable future. This work will also be performed somewhere in Cardiff.

U-Man Zoo

Rock Cottage, Llanbadarn Fawr, Aberystwyth,
Ceredigion SY23 3SG

Tel/*Ffôn*	**+44 (0) 1970 626764**
Fax/*Ffacs*	**+44 (0) 1970 622831**
Email/*Ebost*	**mail@umanzoo.org.uk**
Web/*Y Wê*	**www.umanzoo.org.uk**

Artistic Director/*Cyfarwyddwr Artistig*: **Richard Downing**
Administrator/*Gweinyddydd*: **Janet Roland**

Artistic Policy Polisi Artistig:

To make original performances from original material and to offer these as extraordinary encounters in unorthodox places. To collide, as a matter of process, the experience of practitioners from diverse artistic and cultural backgrounds. To make appeals to the spectator's imagination which are easy to access but dismissed with difficulty. To play seriously.

Company History Hanes y Cwmni:

Formed in 1994 to create 'Motorcity' (a performance upon cars suspended from trees). Over the past 7 years U-Man Zoo has proceeded to make a series of innovative, challenging and widely appealing works at various locations in West Wales working with a core membership of artists drawn from six nations and a broad range of artistic practice. This 'zoo' continues to thrive and develop through the embrace and application of diversity in both process and production.

Past Productions Cynhyrchiadau'r Gorffennol:

Motorcity (1994)**; Vision 20/20** (1996)**; Dome** (1997)**; Kite** (1998)**; The Last Supper** (1999)**; 32 Wardrobes** (2000)**; Wardrobe Residency** (Dublin 2001)**; Water Banquet** (2001)**.**

Future Plans Cynlluniau at y dyfodol:

Water Banquet (Performance/installation), A table of water, 30 feet long and six feet wide; a cyclical but constantly evolving banquet of sound, image and story; of memory, meeting and departure ... and some spoons. following the remarkable reception given to the first serving of Water Banquet at Theatreshop Cymru in October 2001, U-Man Zoo is now preparing to tour the work (within and beyond Wales and the UK) in 2002. Please see the web for details.

"RAIN SCENE, DOME"
Photography Jonathan Clements

Volcano Theatre Company

176 Hanover St, Swansea SA1 6BP

Tel/Ffôn	**+44 (0) 1792 472772**
Fax/Ffacs	**+44 (0) 1792 648230**
Email/Ebost	**volcano.tc@virgin.net**
Web/Y Wê	**www.volcanotheatre.co.uk**

Artistic Directors/*Cyfarwyddwyr Artistig*: **Fern Smith, Paul Davies**
Administrator/*Gweinyddydd*: **Emma Dunton**
General Manager/*Rheolwraig Gyffredinol*
Claudine Conway Assistant/*Cynorthwyydd*

Artistic Policy Polisi Artistig:

For the last 13 years Volcano has produced work which ranges from the adaptation of classic texts to the production of new material generated from within the company. Volcano's reputation for producing high-quality, haunting and provocative physical theatre has made it one of the most challenging and unpredictable companies working in Britain. The objective has always been to confront the complacent, overthrow the orthodox and challenge the conservative.

Company History Hanes y Cwmni:

Founded in1987, Volcano is a national and international touring company committed to a strong audience base in Wales and also to representing the best of Welsh theatre all over the world. Most recently, the company has toured its acclaimed Macbeth: Director's Cut to Dublin and Cork, and to the prestigious Festival Internacional De Teatro Clasico De Almagro in Spain, and plans to take this show to Sri Lanka in February 2001. Macbeth: Director's Cut has also been performed at festivals in Greece, Moscow and Slovakia. The year 2000 has seen a UK-wide tour of Paul Davies' new play Moments of Madness, and also a revival of The Town That Went Mad which was performed at the Homus Novus festival in Riga, Latvia, and also in Kosovo and Albania. Volcano was the first European theatre company to be formally invited to the region after the conflict with Serbia.

The company's educational projects in 2000 included two Summer Schools in Swansea, funded by an 'Arts for All' lottery grant supported by the Swansea Grand Theatre and the Green Futures Eco-Fest. Both Summer Schools culminated in public performances.

Past Productions Cynhyrchiadau'r Gorffennol:

Time of My Life; After the Orgy (1998); **Macbeth, Director's Cut; Moments of Madness; The Town That Went Mad** (1999-2000); **Private Lives; Destination** (2001).

Future Plans Cynlluniau at y dyfodol:

Volcano is planning a co-production with renowned theatre company GRAEAE of Bernhard's **A Party for Boris**, starring Kathryn Hunter and directed by Marcello Magni.

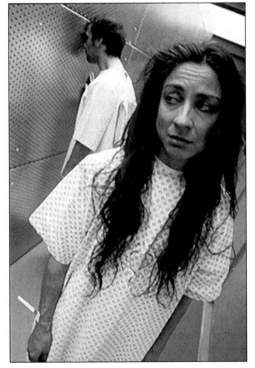

"PRIVATE LIVES" Photography Andrew Jones

Wales Actors' Company

Penallta House, 97 Penallta Rd, Ystrad
Mynach, Hengoed, Caerphilly CF82 7GN

Tel/Ffôn **+44 (0) 1495 271653**
Email/Ebost **garnault@ndirect.co.uk**
Web/Y Wê **www.actors-online.com/**

Artistic Director/Cyfarwyddwr Artistig: **Paul Garnault**
Administrator/Gweinyddydd: **Bill Mason**

Artistic Policy Polisi Artistig:

The Company seeks new approaches to 'Main Stream' theatre and audiences The Company is committed to producing high quality entertaining classical theatre. The Company has an audience base of 10,000 per production. The Company works in an ensemble style allowing greater creative freedom for the actor. The emphasis is put on the creativity of the stage actor and the physical and visual power of the text, rather than the technical paraphernalia behind which many a production is obscured. As well as pioneering new venues and audiences in Wales with its open air and community productions it has a 90% local casting policy with a commitment to developing new actors.

Company History Hanes y Cwmni:

Founded in 1985. It is known mainly for its classical open air productions, such as **Romeo and Juliet, King Lear, A Midsummer Nights Dream, Othello, The Tempest, Cymbeline, As You Like It, Macbeth, Much Ado About Nothing, Julius Caesar, Twelfth Night, Hamlet, Henry V, Romeo and Juliet**, which all toured nationally. The Company also produced various touring productions such as **Doctor Faustus, Rosencrantz and Guildenstern are Dead, The Sin Eaters, Testament of Youth, Germinal** and **Shirley Valentine.**

Past Productions Cynhyrchiadau'r Gorffennol:

Tissue; Romeo and Juliet (1985)**; King Lear; Doctor Faustus** (1986)**; Rosencrantz and Guildenstern are Dead** (1987)**; A Midsummer Night's Dream** (1988)**; Othello** (1989)**; The Tempest** (1990)**; Cymbeline** (1991)**; As You Like It** (1992)**; Macbeth; The Sin Eaters** (1993)**; Much Ado About Nothing; Testament of Youth; Germinal** (1994)**; Julius Caesar; Shirley Valentine** (1995)**; Twelfth Night** (1996)**; Hamlet** (1997)**; Henry V** (1998)**; Romeo and Juliet** (1999)**; Juno and the Paycock; Midsummer Nights Dream** (2000)**; Macbeth** (2001)**.**

Future Plans Cynlluniau at y dyfodol:

To remain independent and build its audience base.

Welsh Fargo Stage Company

166 Llandaff Rd, Cardiff CF11 9PX

Tel/Ffôn   **+44 (0) 29 2039 5078**
Fax/Ffacs   **+44 (0) 29 2034 0892**
Email/Ebost   **Mgsmkelly@aol.com**

Artistic Director/CyfarwyddwrArtistig: **Michael Kelligan**

Artistic Policy Polisi Artistig:

One man performances by Michael Kelligan. Small-scale touring of new and extant dramas.

Company History Hanes y Cwmni:

The Company was formed to present The Spirit of Enniskellen based on a story by Gordon Wilson with Alf McCleary.

Future Plans Cynlluniau at y dyfodol:

Michael Emlyn's Dylan, a restaging of an Emlyn Wlliams play.

Venues

CANOLFANNAU

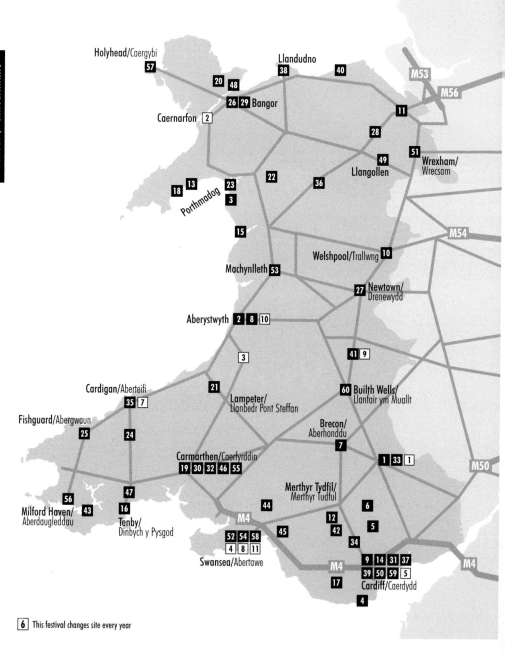

Holyhead/Caergybi
57

Llandudno
38   40

M53

M56

20   48

26 29 Bangor

M11

Caernarfon 2

28

49   51

Wrexham/
Wrecsam

Llangollen

18   13   23   3

22   36

Porthmadog

M54

15

Welshpool/Trallwng 10

Machynlleth 53

Newtown/
Drenewydd

27

Aberystwyth 2 8 10

3

41 9

Cardigan/Aberteifi

21

60 Builth Wells/
Llanfair ym Muallt

35 7

Lampeter/
Llanbedr Pont Steffan

Fishguard/Abergwaun

Brecon/
Aberhonddu

25   24

7

1 33 1

M50

Carmarthen/Caerfyrddin

19 30 32 46 55

Merthyr Tydfil/
Merthyr Tudful

56   47

44

6

Milford Haven/
Aberdaugleddau

43   16

12   5

Tenby/
Dinbych y Pysgod

42

34

52 54 58

45

9 14 31 37

M4

4 8 11

39 50 59 5

Swansea/Abertawe

M4

Cardiff/Caerdydd

17

M4

4

6 This festival changes site every year

1 Theatr y Fwrdeistref
Y Fenni / Abergavenny
Borough Theatre
Town Hall, Cross St, Abergavenny,
Monmouthshire NP7 5EU

Tel/*Ffôn*	**+44 (0) 1873 850805** box office
	+44 (0) 1873 735830 admin
Fax/*Ffacs*	**+44 (0) 1873 858083**
Email/*Ebost*	**boroughtheatre@monmouthshire.gov.uk**

Administrator/*Gweinyddydd*: **Nick Banwell**
Technical Contact/*Cyswllt Technegol*: **Ioan Wynne** 07768 146341

Technical Details Manylion Technegol:
Situated on 3rd floor of town hall. Lifts available. Seating - 338.

Disabled resources and access
Adnoddau a mynediad i'r anabl:
Access via lift. Toilets. Seating at the front of the stalls.

Artistic Policy Polisi Artistig:
All forms of music, dance, drama and opera. Can negotiate fees, split, first call etc. Theatre not available for hire to commercial managements.

2 Canolfan y Celfyddydau
Aberystwyth Arts Centre
University of Wales, Aberystwyth
Ceredigion SY23 3DE

Tel/*Ffôn*	**+44 (0) 1970 622882**
Fax/*Ffacs*	**+44 (0) 1970 622883**
Email/*Ebost*	**gld@aber.ac.uk**
Web/*Y Wê*	**www.aber.ac.uk/artscentre**

Artistic Director/*Cyfarwyddwr Artistig*: **Alan Hewson**
Deputy Director/*Dirprwy Gyfarwyddwr*: **Louise Amery**
Technical Manager/*Rheolwr Technegol*: **Wyn Jones**
Performing Arts Officer/*Swyddog y Celfyddau Perfformio*: **Gill Ogden**
Administrator/*Gweinyddydd*: **Maris Davies**

Technical Details Manylion Technegol:
Theatre/*Theatr* - Stage: Open ended/pros. Pros 6m high x 11m wide Access: dock door 5.53m x 2.30m; Seating - 321 (flexible).
Great Hall/*Neuadd Fawr* - Very adaptable space for varied events; Seating - 1250.
Studio/*Stwdio* - 12m circular space, sprung floor; Seating - 120 (flexible).
Cinema/*Sinema* - Seating - 125.
Foyer/*Cyntedd* - Perf. spaces up to 300 capacity.

Disabled resources and access
Adnoddau a mynediad i'r anabl:
The venue is fully accessible at all levels by lift or stairlift. Access ramps, low level phones, wheelchair spaces in all auditoria. Toilets on each floor. Parking adjacent to the building.

Mae llifftiau neu llifftiau grisiau'n mynd i bob llawr yn y Ganolfan. Ceir yma rampiau, teleffonau isel ac mae lle i gadeiriau olwyn yn yr holl awditoria. Mae gennym doiledau i'r anabl ar bob llawr a lle i bobl anabl barcio ger yr adeilad

Artistic Policy Polisi Artistig:
Aberystwyth Arts Centre is the main venue for the arts in Mid Wales. It aims to provide a wide ranging, involving and fully accessible experience of the arts to all sections of the community in the context of a bilingual and bicultural community.
Recently redeveloped as part of a major £3.6 million project (completed April 2000) the venue is respected nationally as a 'flagship for the arts', and has facilities unrivalled throughout Wales and much of the UK. It houses a theatre, concert hall, cinema, studio, a wealth of purpose - built workshop spaces, exhibition galleries, plus all the facilities you would expect in a major arts venue such as cafe, bars, craftshop and bookshop.
The Arts Centre presents well over 400 performances a year, plus a busy cinema programme and an internationally renowned exhibition programme. A busy timetable of community/education workshops and courses attract over 46,000 participants a year. Although predominantly a presenting venue, the Arts Centre does produce its own shows throughout the year, including a successful summer season and in-house community productions. Presents a number of prestigious festivals in many different art forms, and is involved in co-promotions and collaborations with leading companies and organisations.

Canolfan y Celfyddydau yw prif ganolfan gelfyddydol Canolbarth Cymru. Ei nod yw cynnig profiad eang, cynhwysol a hygyrch o'r celfyddydau i bob rhan o'r gymuned ddwyieithog a dauddiwylliant y mae'n rhan ohoni. Adeiladwyd y Ganolfan tua dechrau'r 1970au ac fe'i hailddatblygwyd yn ddiweddar fel rhan o brosiect mawr gwerth £4 miliwn a gwblhawyd ym mis Ebrill 2000.

Mae'r Ganolfan yn un o brif ganolfannau celfyddydau'r wlad ac mae'r cyfleusterau heb eu hail yng Nghymru na llawer o weddill Prydain. Ceir yma theatr, neuadd gyngerdd, sinema, stiwdio, llu o ystafelloedd gweithdy pwrpasol, orielau arddangos, a'r holl gyfleusterau y byddech yn disgwyl eu gweld mewn canolfan gelfyddydau o bwys, fel caffi, bariau, siop grefftau a siop lyfrau.

Mae Canolfan y Celfyddydau yn cyflwyno ymhell dros 400 o berfformiadau y flwyddyn, ceir yma raglen brysur yn y sinema ac mae'r orielau arddangos yn denu pobl o bell ac agos. Mae dros 45,000 o bobl y flwyddyn yn cymryd rhan mewn gweithdai a chyrsiau cymunedol ac addysgol. Er mai cyflwyno gwaith perfformwyr o sefydliadau allanol a wneir yma yn bennaf, mae Canolfan y Celfyddydau yn cynhyrchu ei sioeau ei hunan, yn cynnwys sioe haf lwyddiannus a chynyrchiadau cymunedol. Cynhelir nifer o wyliau celfyddydol amrywiol yma ac mae'r Ganolfan yn cydweithio'n aml â chwmnïau a sefydliadau blaenllaw.

❸ Theatr Ardudwy

Harlech LL46 2PU

Tel/*Ffôn* **+44 (0) 1766 780667**
Fax/*Ffacs* **+44 (0) 1766 780778**
Email/*Ebost* **gwynl.theatrardudwy@virgin.net**
Web/*Y Wê* **www.lokalink.co.uk/harlech/**
theatre_ardudwy/index.htm

Artistic Director/*Cyfarwyddwr Artistig*: **Mici Plwm** & administrator/*gweinyddydd*:
Technical Contact/*Cyswllt Technegol*: **David Evans**

Technical Details Manylion Technegol:

Stage: front of apron to curtain line 3.5m; curtain line to rear surround 6.4m; front of apron to screen tabs 6m (half stage depth). Width at curtain line 13.1m; max. width DS of curtain 13.5m; pros: max. height 5.63m; min. height 4.72m. Seating - 266 .

Disabled resources and access
Adnoddau a mynediad i'r anabl:

Currently under improvement.

Artistic Policy Polisi Artistig:

Mixed programme of drama, dance, opera, concerts, light entertainment, films and pantomime. The theatre has a bilingual policy in Welsh and English.

❹ Barry Memorial Hall

The Memorial Hall Theatre, Gladstone Rd, Barry, South Glamorgan CF64 8NA

Tel/*Ffôn* **+44 (0) 1446 738663**
Email/*Ebost* **katelong@barrymemo.fsnet.co.uk**
Artistic Director/*Cyfarwyddwr Artistig*: **Kate Long**

Technical Details Manylion Technegol:

Pros; performing area 11.95m x 8.62m. No rake - floor wood suitable for dance (not barefoot), Backstage Crossover. Stage not heated.

Disabled resources and access
Adnoddau a mynediad i'r anabl:

Backstage not accessible to disabled performers and staff.

❺ Blackwood Miners Institute

High St, Blackwood NP12 1BB

Tel/*Ffôn* **+44 (0) 1495 224425**
+44 (0) 1495 227206
Fax/*Ffacs* **+44 (0) 1495 226457**

Administrator/*Gweinyddydd*: **Carol Thomas**
Technical Contact/*Cyswllt Technegol*: **Robin Bainbridge**

Technical Details Manylion Technegol:

Stage: pros 7.18m x 4.20m; perf. area 8.1m x 6m (incl. apron). Dance studio - sprung floor.

Disabled resources and access
Adnoddau a mynediad i'r anabl:

Ramped entrance, lift with low level buttons, level access auditorium, bar, restaurant. Wheelchair accessible toilets, seats in auditorium. Guide dogs welcome. Backstage not accessible for disabled performers and staff.

VENUES / CANOLFANNAU

6 The Beaufort Theatre

Beaufort Hill, Beaufort, Ebbw Vale, Blaenau
Gwent NP23 5QQ

Tel/Ffôn	+44 (0) 1495 302112
	+44 (0) 1495 307354 box office
Fax/Ffacs	+44 (0) 1495 308996
Email/Ebost	beaufort.theatre@virgin.net
Web/Y Wê	www.beauforttheatre.com

Arts Development Manager/*Rheolwr Datblygu'r Celfyddydau*:**Richard Hughes**
Marketing Officer/*Swyddog Marchnata*: **Lynsey Wheeler**
Administrator/*Gweinyddydd*: **Ceri Caffey**
Technical Contact/Cyswllt Technegol: **Dave Bevan**

Technical Details Manylion Technegol:

Pros 5.7m wide; Stage 7.6m, 6m (min.). Seating - Theatre 360; Ballroom 150.

Disabled resources and access Adnoddau a mynediad i'r anabl:

Level access, designated wheelchair bay in the theatre, Toilets. Induction loop in theatre. Access between theatre and ballroom difficult for those with mobility problems.

Artistic Policy Polisi Artistig:

The Beaufort Theatre programmes professional theatre, music, contemporary dance and light entertainment. The theatre is also host to nine voluntary arts organisations who present their annual productions here.

History Hanes:

The Beaufort Theatre is an ACW core venue; a member of PAG and ITC.

Future Plans Cynlluniau at y dyfodol:

With the aid of an ACW lottery grant new seats for theatre to be installed by August 2001. New PA system for the theatre and ballroom will also be purchased. The theatre aims to develop the links between the 'Valleys Roots' venues and to gain a Barclays News Stage Partners award in partnership with Theatr Brycheiniog, Gwent Theatre and the Borough Theatre.

7 Theatr Brycheiniog

Canal Wharf, Brecon, Powys LD3 7EW

Tel/Ffôn	+44 (0) 1874 622838
Fax/Ffacs	+44 (0) 1874 622583
Email/Ebost	andy@brycheiniog.co.uk

Artistic Director & Administrator/
Cyfarwyddwyr Artistig a Gweinyddydd: **Andy Eagle**
Technical Contact/Cyswllt Technegol: **Geraint Thomas**

Technical Details Manylion Technegol:

Stage: 14.5m wide x 12.3m deep (with pit 15.3m) x 11.1m high (not a full height fly tower). 2 get-ins, one street level via workshop, one lorry height straight to stage. 4 dressing rooms, 1 rehearsal studio/conference room (150 people). Seating 477 flexible, cabaret/stand up.

Disabled resources and access Adnoddau a mynediad i'r anabl:

Level access/lifts to all public areas. Toilets. Spaces for wheelchair users in stalls and balcony. Infra red hearing system. Guide dogs welcome. Reserved parking. Information available in large print.

Artistic Policy Polisi Artistig:

To provide multi-purpose spaces for use by professional touring companies, the community and voluntary groups. To present quality theatre, dance, opera, concerts, exhibitions, conferences and is one of the venues for the very successful Brecon Jazz Festival.

8 Theatr Y Castell

St Michael's Pl, Aberystwyth SY23 1DE

Tel/Ffôn	+44 (0) 1970 624606
Fax/Ffacs	+44 (0) 1970 622831

Technical Contact/*Cysywllt Technegol*: **Richard Downing** 01970 626764

9 Chapter (Cardiff) Ltd

Chapter Arts Centre, Market Rd, Canton,
Cardiff CF5 7QE

Tel/Ffôn   **+44 (0) 29 2031 1050**
Fax/Ffacs   **+44 (0) 29 2031 3431**
Email/Ebost   **enquiry@chapter.org**
Web/Y Wê   **www.chapter.org**

Artistic Directors/Cyfarwyddwyr Artistig: **Janek Alexander**
Theatre Programmer/Rhaglennydd Theatr: **James Tyson**
Publicity Officer/Swyddog Cyhoeddusrwydd: **Carol Jones**
House Manager/Rheolwr y Neuadd: **Graham Shelswell** ,
Administrator/Gweinyddydd: **Judi Newton**

Technical Details Manylion Technegol:

Stage: 8.75m wide x 9.75m (max 14.5m) deep x 3.8m high. Access: stairs or
lift.

Disabled resources and access Adnoddau a mynediad i'r anabl:

Full access (lift and ground floor access into building).

Artistic Policy Polisi Artistig:

To present and produce high quality contemporary performing arts from Britain
and the world.

10 Theatr Clera

Salop Rd, Welshpool SY21 7RE

Tel/Ffôn   **+44 (0) 1938 554378** answerphone
             +44 (0) 1938 552014 manned
Fax/Ffacs   **+44 (0) 1938 555711**
Email/Ebost   **info@theatrclera.co.uk**
Web/Y Wê   **www.theatrclera.co.uk**

Administrator/Gweinyddydd: **Kay Jones**
Technical Contact/Cyswllt Technegol: **Mark Bardsley**

Technical Details Manylion Technegol:

Seating - 314 in raked and link seating.

Disabled resources and access Adnoddau a mynediad i'r anabl:

Good facilities for the disabled. Wheelchair access is good. Toilet.

Artistic Policy Polisi Artistig:

The theatre gives opportunity for the rural community to enjoy many kinds of
theatre at its best, with professional companies regularly staging performances.
It is also a venue for the people of the area to stage their own productions, with
the help of professional staff at the theatre.

11 Clwyd Theatr Cymru

County Civic Centre, Mold CH7 1YA

Tel/Ffôn   **+44 (0) 1352 755114** box office
Fax/Ffacs   **+44 (0) 1352 752323**
Email/Ebost   **info@clwyd-theatr-cymru.co.uk**
Web/Y Wê   **www.clwyd-theatr-cymru.co.uk/**

Director/Cyfarwyddwr: **Terry Hands**
Associate Director/Cyfarwyddwr Cyswllt: **Tim Baker**
General Manager/Rheolwraig Gyffredinol: **Chris Ricketts**
Finance Controller/Rheolwraig Cyllid: **Julia Grime**
Production Manager/Rheolwr Cynhyrchu: **Bob Irwin**
Marketing Manager/Rheolwraig Marchnata: **Ann Williams**
Sponsorship Manager/Rheolwraig Nawdd: **Annie Dayson**
Technical-Development Manager/Rheolwr Technegol a Datblygu: **Pat Nelder**

Technical Details Manylion Technegol:

Anthony Hopkins Theatre Pros. stage; opening 10.65m x 6.5m high
(variable). Seating - 534.
Emlyn Williams Theatre Flexible studio. Upholstered seating on steeldeck
rostra, flexible. Seating - 150-250.
TV Studio Former TV studio, rehearsals/small scale performance.
The Clwyd Room Space: 15m x 11m. Sprung wooden floor.

Disabled resources and access Adnoddau a mynediad i'r anabl:

Wheelchair access via a ramp at main entrance. Designated parking. Staff on
hand to help. Inform Box Office of requirements. Lift to all floors, Toilets on all
levels, wheelchair spaces, induction loop system in all venues.

Artistic Policy Polisi Artistig:

Built as an Arts Centre in 1976, Clwyd Theatr Cymru is the home of the highly
acclaimed producing company which presents most of its work on tour
throughout Wales. The theatre also hosts a variety of touring drama, dance,
music and a community Festival in the Summer.
*Adeiladwyd fel canolfan celfyddydau ym 1976. Mae Clwyd Theatr Cymru yn gartref i
gwmni cynhyrchu o'r safon uchaf sy'n cyflwyno'i mwyafrif o'u gwaith ar daith led-led
Cymru. Yn ogystal mae'r theatr yn cynnal amrywiaeth o ddramâu teithio, dawns,
cerddoriaeth a gŵyl gymunedol yn yr haf.*

12 The Coliseum

Mount Pleasant St, Trecynon, Aberdare,
Rhondda Cynon Taff, CF44 8NG

Tel/Ffôn   **+44 (0) 1685 881188**
Fax/Ffacs   **+44 (0) 1685 883000**
Email/Ebost   **info@coliseum-aberdare.co.uk**
Web/Y Wê   **www.coliseum-aberdare.co.uk**

Artistic Director/Cyfarwyddwr Artistig: **Adrian Williams**

Disabled resources and access
Adnoddau a mynediad i'r anabl:

Cinema: The stalls area has induction loops. Contact us via our minicom, our number is 883769. Ramp access to foyer, toilet facilities, lifts from stalls to bar. 10 wheelchair spaces with companion seats. Guide dogs welcome.

Artistic Policy Polisi Artistig:

A civic theatre with a lively mixed programme of cinema and live shows. Other performances include opera, contemporary dance, ballet and orchestral concerts. The Coliseum Theatre was originally opened in 1938. Since then it has played host to many celebrities and is also the place to see ballet, opera, drama and dance. The Coliseum also provides a platform for many local schools and amateur-dramatic organisations to perform. The Coliseum is also home to the newly formed Drama Academy. We do pay guarantees but prefer to take shows on a first-call or box-office split. The venue is also available to hire.

14 St David's Hall

St David's Hall, The Hayes, Cardiff CF10 1SH

Tel/Ffôn   **+44 (0) 29 2087 8420**
Fax/Ffacs   **+44 (0) 29 2087 8599**
Email/Ebost   **J.Hill@cardiff.gov.uk**

General Manager/Rheolwraig Gyffredinol: **Tony Williams**
Technical Manager/Rheolwr Technegol: **Simon Denman**

Technical Details Manylion Technegol:

Stage: standard 10.8m x 17.3m; maximum 16.6m x 17.3m; suspension facilities over stage. Seating - 2,000. 750 at stall level, 350 rear of the platform, 900 in tiers.

Disabled resources and access
Adnoddau a mynediad i'r anabl:

Special level entrance with automatic doors, braille lift plates, wheelchair positions in auditorium, hearing induction loop.

Artistic Policy Polisi Artistig:

Considered one of the finest concert halls of its size in Europe with the very best acoustics, St David's Hall offers a varied programme including classical music from world-famous orchestras, internationally famous soloists, choral and organ music, pop, rock, jazz, folk, dance, indoor spectator sports, film shows, fashion spectaculars, lectures and ceremonies and regular lunchtime recitals.

13 Criccieth Memorial Hall

Tel/Ffôn   **+44 (0) 1766 522986**

Artistic Policy Polisi Artistig:

Plays, pantomimes, concerts and recitals are held regularly.

15 Dragon Theatre
Theatr y Ddraig

Barmouth, Gwynedd LL43 2AR

Tel/Ffôn   **+44 (0) 1341 280392**

Manager/Rheolwr: **Harrison Wilde**

Technical Details Manylion Technegol:

Community Centre. Pros. Arch. Performing area 8.53m x 6.1m. Pros.opening 8.53m x 3.65m. No rake - floor covered wood. Suitable for all dance. Harlequin dance floor available. No permanent staff, casuals available. Seating - 205, retractable.

Disabled resources and access
Adnoddau a mynediad i'r anabl:

6 wheel chair spaces - ground level entrance, lift to stalls. Induction loop. Toilet.

16 De Valence Pavilion

Upper Frog St, Tenby SA70 7JD

Tel/Ffôn **+44 (0) 1834 842730** + fax/ffacs

Artistic Director/Cyfarwyddwr Artistig: **Kay Philips**

Technical Details Manylion Technegol:

Pros. Arch: 9.14m x 3.35m. Seating - 500 (Stacking Chairs).

Artistic Policy Polisi Artistig:

Theatre - Any form of entertainment would be considered.

17 St Donats Arts Centre

St Donats Castle, Vale of Glamorgan CF61 1WF

Tel/Ffôn **+44 (0) 1446 799099**
Fax/Ffacs **+44 (0) 1446 799101**
Email/Ebost **boxoffice@stdonats.com**
Web/Y Wê **www.stdonats.com/**

Artistic Director/Cyfarwyddwr Artistig: **David Ambrose** 01446 799095
Administrator/Gweinyddydd: **Sharon Stone** 01446 799104
Technical Contact/Cyswllt Technegol: **Leigh Morgan** 01446 799098

Technical Details Manylion Technegol:

Tythe Barn: End on performing area 7.6m x 6.1m. Seating - 230
Bradenstoke Hall: Flat floor 24.4m x 7.9m, plus stage 4.57m x 7.9m, seating/performance area flexible. Height to apex 20m. Seating - 330.

Artistic Policy Polisi Artistig:

In the grounds of a S. Wales medieval castle, the Arts Centre's dramatic location offers inspiration to artists, and a memorable experience for its many visitors from all over the world. The Centre runs a professional public theatre, converted from a medieval Tythe Barn in the 70s. Two seasons: Varied programme theatre, music, dance, films, exhibitions in the Tythe Barn Theatre, Oct-April; Summer Season of large, (mainly outdoor) festivals May-September.

18 Neuadd Dwyfor

Cinema/Theatre

Stryd Penlan, Pwllheli, Gwynedd LL53 5DN

Tel/Ffôn **+44 (0) 1758 704088**

Manager/Rheolwr: **Ann Rowena Jones**

Technical Details Manylion Technegol:

Pros: 9.14m x 7.6m. Seating - 345 raked circle/stalls.

Artistic Policy Polisi Artistig:

Welsh/English drama, professional dance companies, opera, concerts and puppets. Available for hire and Amateur Shows.

19 Theatr Elli

Llanelli Entertainment Centre, Station Rd, Llanelli, Carmarthen SA15 1AH

Tel/Ffôn **+44 (0) 1554 752659**

Artistic Director/Cyfarwyddwr Artistig: **Carwyn Rogers**

Technical Details Manylion Technegol:

Seating: Theatr Elli, raked - 487, Theatre 2 - 330.

20 Theatr Fach

Pencraig, Llangefni, Anglesey

Tel/Ffôn **+44 (0) 1248 722412**

General Secretary/Ysgrifennydd Cyffredinol: **Mrs A S Davies**

Technical Details Manylion Technegol:

Seating - 110.

Artistic Policy Polisi Artistig:

Bi-lingual plays, pantomime, etc, for the rural community.

21 Canolfan Addysg Gymunedol, Theatr Felinfach

Dyffryn Aeron, Ceredigion SA48 8AF

Tel/Ffôn   **+44 (0) 1570 470697**
Fax/Ffacs   **+44 (0) 1570 471030**
Email/Ebost   **swyddfa@theatrfelinfach.demon.co.uk**
Web/Y Wê   **www.theatrfelinfach.demon.co.uk**

Lecturer in Charge/Darlithydd mewn Gofal: **Dwynwen Lloyd Raggett**
Administrator/Gweinyddydd: **Melinda Williams**
Technical Contact/Cyswllt Technegol: **Dylan Williams**

Technical Details Manylion Technegol:
Seating - 263

Disabled resources and access Adnoddau a mynediad i'r anabl:
Mynediad di-rwystr un-lefel ar gyfer defnyddwyr cadeirau olwyn. Eisteddlleoedd neilltuol ar gyfer cadeiriau olwyn yn yr awditoriwm.

Artistic Policy Polisi Artistig:
Creu cyfleoedd addysgol i blant a phobl ifanc yn arbennig, a'r gymuned yn gyffredinol, trwy gyfrwng y celfyddydau perfformiadol a gweledol yn arbennig ynghyd â chyfryngau radio, ffilm a theledu. Gweithredir y polisi hwn ar sail Drws Agored a thrwy gyfrwng y diwylliant cynhenid.

22 Ffestiniog Village Hall

Village Square, Ffestiniog, Gwynedd LL41 4LG

Tel/Ffôn   **+44 (0) 1766 762782**

Artistic Director/Cyfarwyddwr Artistig: **Emma Ayres**

Technical Details Manylion Technegol:
Stage: 6.54m x 3.96m. Seating - 240.

23 Y Ganolfan

Porthmadog, High St, Porthmadog LL49 9LU

Tel/Ffôn   **+44 (0) 1766 513372**

Technical Details Manylion Technegol:
Seating - 400 (Village Hall).

24 Theatr Y Gromlech

Preseli Community Education Centre, Crymych, Sir Benfro SA41 3QH

Tel/Ffôn   **+44 (0) 1239 831455**
Fax/Ffacs   **+44 (0) 1239 831964**
Email/Ebost   **prescomed@hotmail.com**

Artistic Directors/Cyfarwyddwyr Artistig:
David Hedley Williams, Eleri Mai Thomas

Technical Details Manylion Technegol:
The theatre is located in a school/community centre. Seating - 208 (raked).

Disabled resources and access Adnoddau a mynediad i'r anabl:
Disabled resources and access good.

Artistic Policy Polisi Artistig:
Primarily Welsh language productions, those with a Welsh connection, or that are relevant to the area and the community of north Pembrokeshire.

25 Theatr Gwaun

Y Wesh, Abergwaun, Sir Benfo/
West St, Fishguard, Pembrokeshire SA65 9AD

Tel/Ffôn   **+44 (0) 1348 873421**
Fax/Ffacs   **+44 (0) 1348 872694**

Manager/Rheolwr: **Melanie Lucking**

Technical Details Manylion Technegol:
Stage Pros. W 5.2m x D 4.5m. Full pa + Soundcraft 16 mixing desk. 4 off strand lighting ACT6 DMX. 40 lanterns available. Seating 188 raked.

Disabled resources and access Adnoddau a mynediad i'r anabl:
Ramps from the street. 4 wheelchair spaces, induction loop. Toilets. Guide dogs welcome; one staff member is stage one signer.

Artistic Policy Polisi Artistig:
A multi-purpose arts venue providing and promoting a programme of performing arts including cinema, drama and music. It is available for hire by community and commercial groups. Exhibition space is also available.

26 Theatr Gwynedd

Ffordd Deiniol, Bangor, Gwynedd LL57 2TL

Tel/Ffôn **+44 (0) 1248 351707**
Fax/Ffacs **+44 (0) 1248 351915**
Email/Ebost **theatr@theatrgwynedd.co.uk**
Web/Y Wê **www.theatrgwynedd.com**

Director/Cyfarwyddwr: **Dafydd Thomas**
Artistic Director/Cyfarwyddwr Artistig: **Ian Rowlands**
Deputy Director/Dirprwy Gyfarwyddwr: **Ann Evans**
Marketing & Sales Officer/Swyddog Marchnata a Gwerthiant: **Fiona Otting**

Technical Details Manylion Technegol:

Stage: open end with pros. With Apron; pros. width 12.8m max; 9.6m normal; Pros
.height 5.7m max; 5.2m normal; Stage width 16.1m max; Stage depth 10.3m max. to
back wall; 9.25m normal (with Cyc); Apron depth 2.75m; Stage to fly floor 6.3m
(clearance); Stage to grid (flying) 13.9m; Orchestra pit approx 35 players; Depth of pit
2.44m; Seating 348.
*Llwyfan ben agored gyda pros. Gyda blaen llwyfan. Lled pros ar ei fwyaf 12.8m arferol
9.6m; Uchder y pros ar ei fwyaf 5.7m, arferol 5.2m. Lled y llwyfan ar ei fwyaf 16.1m.
Dyfnder y llwyfan i'r wal gefn 10.3m; arferol gyda. Seiclorama 9.25m; dyfnder blaen
llwyfan 2.75m. Uchder o'r llwyfan i'r briglofft 6.3m. Uchder o'r llwyfan i'r grid 13.9m.
Corlan y gerddorfa - lle i 35, dyfnder y gorlan 2.44m. Awditoriwm - 348 sedd.*

Disabled resources and access
Adnoddau a mynediad i'r anabl:

Ramped access to the auditorium, bar, box office. Toilets in bar area. Hearing
loop for film only. Theatre programme available on tape/bold print. Parking
available booking recommended.
*Rampiau yn rhoi mynediad i'r swyddfa docynnau, bar a'r awditoriwm. Toiledau ar gyfer yr
anabl yn y bar. Dolen glyw ar gyfer ffilmiau yn unig. Ar hyn o bryd. Rhaglen y Theatr ar
gael ar dâp neu mewn print bras. Parcio ar gyfer pobl anabl, rhaid archebu o flaen llaw.*

Artistic Policy Polisi Artistig:

The Theatre's main aim is to provide a complete theatre service for the local area
(Gwynedd, Anglesey, Conwy). Its location at the centre of the most populated part of
the area allows the Theatre and its staff to deal with: Productions that are brought
in, be they Welsh or English dramas as well as presentations of opera, dance,
concerts and films; Stage events of every kind eminating from the local community;
Cwmni Theatr Gwynedd's productions. Theatr Gwynedd is the home of Cwmni Theatr
Gwynedd, the only Welsh language company located in its own theatre.
*Prif nod Theatr Gwynedd yw darparu gwasanaeth theatr cyflawn ar gyfer dalgylch lleol
(Gwynedd, Ynys Môn, Conwy). Oherwydd ei safle yng nghanol yr ardal fwyaf poblog o'r
dalgylch, gall y Theatr a'i staff ymdrin yn effeithiol gyda: Y cynyrchiadau a gaiff eu prynu i
mewn, yn ddramâu Cymraeg a Saesneg, ynghyd a chyflwyniadau dawns, opera,
cyngherddau a ffilmiau. Digwyddiadau llwyfan o bob math sy'n tarddu neu'n rhan o'r
gymuned leol. Gweithgaredd Cwmni Theatr Gwynedd gyda'i ymroddiad i gyflwyno gwaith
Llwyfan o'r radd flaenaf yn yr iaith Gymraeg. Theatr Gwynedd yw cartref Cwmni Theatr
Gwynedd, yr unig gwmni theatr Cymraeg sydd wedi ei leoli mewn Theatr ei hun.*

27 Theatr Hafren

Llanidloes Rd, Newtown, Powys SY16 4HU

Tel/Ffôn **+44 (0) 1686 625447**
Fax/Ffacs **+44 (0) 1686 625446**
Email/Ebost **admin@theatrhafren.co.uk**
Web/Y Wê **www.theatrhafren.co.uk**

Administrator/Gweinyddydd: **Sara Clutton**
Technical Contact/Cyswllt Technegol: **Peter Whitehead**

Technical Details Manylion Technegol:

Stage approx: 12m wide x 8m deep x 5m high. SL wings approx 2m, SR wings
7m. No fly-tower. Loading-bay door leads straight onto SR wings. Access good
for all types of transport. Bay width 2.5m, lifting height from outside ground
level 1m, doors 3.5m high. Seating: auditorium 508-548. Audiences 400+
no forestage. 2 fixed balconies. Seating unit of 384 seats can be withdrawn -
clear floor area 12m x 12m. 125 loose seats available.

Disabled resources and access
Adnoddau a mynediad i'r anabl:

Full disabled parking, access and facilities.

28 Theatr John Ambrose, Canolfan Glyndwr

Ysgol Brynhyfryd, Mold Rd, Ruthin LL15 1EG

Tel/Ffôn **+44 (0) 1824 703933**

Administrator/Gweinyddydd: **John Bennett Jones**

Technical Details Manylion Technegol:

Stage: pros. 9.98m x 5.8m, 4.09m high; Grid 5.17m high; Seating 200 (+170).

Disabled resources and access
Adnoddau a mynediad i'r anabl:

Via back-stage lift; Hearing induction loop.

29 John Phillips Hall

The Normal College, Bangor,
Gwynedd LL57 2DG

Tel/Ffôn   +44 (0) 1248 3510140 / 370171
Fax/Ffacs   +44 (0) 1248 370461

Artistic Director/Cyfarwyddwr Artistig: **Geoffrey Lincoln**

Technical Details Manylion Technegol:

Pros: 14.02m x 6.7m. Seating - 400.

Artistic Policy Polisi Artistig:

Music & theatre - Mainly orchestral concerts; small/medium scale touring.

30 Llandovery Theatre

Stone St, Llandovery, Carmarthen SA20 0DP

Tel/Ffôn   **+44 (0) 1550 720113**

Artistic Directors/Cyfarwyddwyr Artistig: **Jacqueline Harrison, Simon Barnes**
Technical Contact/Cyswllt Technegol: **Simon Barnes**

Technical Details Manylion Technegol:

6.7m deep x 8.5m wide. Seating - 150.

Artistic Policy Polisi Artistig:

Junior drama workshops; school productions; own productions; open to offers.

31 Llanover Hall Theatre

Romilly Rd, Canton, Cardiff CF15 1FH

Tel/Ffôn   **+44 (0) 29 2063 1144**
Fax/Ffacs   **+44 (0) 29 2063 1142**
Email/Ebost **office@llanover.org**
Web/Y Wê   **www.llanover.org**

Contact/Cyswllt: **Stuart H Bawler**

Technical Details Manylion Technegol:

Studio: 18m x 9m x 4.5m (to rig); Moveable flexible seating - 100.

Disabled resources and access Adnoddau a mynediad i'r anabl:

Ramps and lifts to all floors.

Artistic Policy Polisi Artistig:

Home to Shining Wits productions and three prolific youth theatre groups. Open access to all. Specialises in community and young people's performances. Open to professional and amateur companies.

32 Lyric Theatre

King St, Carmarthen SA31 1DQ

Tel/Ffôn   **+44 (0) 1267 232632** box
             +44 (0) 1267 238685 admin
Email/Ebost **Anything@lyric.freeserve.co.uk**
Web/Y Wê   **www.carmarthonline.co.uk/lyric**

Artistic Director/Cyfarwyddwr Artistig: **Elizabeth Evans** MBE
             01267 236853 / Elizabeth@Lizevans.co.uk
Technical Contact/Cyswllt Technegol: **David Evans**
             01267 236853 / David@daievans.com

Technical Details Manylion Technegol:

Pros. 9.68m wide x 6.4m high, grid height 15m racked; stage 1 in 70 back to front, stage 11m deep, Orchestra pit 90 sq m, Full fly tower 34 no lines counter balanced, Access direct to stage via back lane. Seating 740.

Disabled resources and access Adnoddau a mynediad i'r anabl:

Access from disabled parking bay outside to stalls. 20 numbered wheelchair spaces. Infra red sound system for the hard of hearing.

Artistic Policy Polisi Artistig:

To promote the arts among youngsters in the Carmarthen and district.

33 The Melville Theatre

The Drama Centre, Pen-y-Pound,
Abergavenny, Monmouthshire NP7 5UD

Tel/Ffôn   **+44 (0) 1873 853167**
Email/Ebost   **gwenttie@aol.com**
Web/Y Wê   **www.gwenttie.co.uk**

Artistic Director/Cyfarwyddwr Artistig: **Gary Meredith**
Administrator/Gweinyddydd: **Julia Davies**

Technical Details Manylion Technegol:

Stage: 6.9m wide, 6.5m deep, Grid height 4.2m. 1 entrance to stage through fire door stage right. 2x13A sockets. No resident technician. Seating - 75.

Disabled resources and access Adnoddau a mynediad i'r anabl:

Parking spaces lead to well-lit access for wheelchair users. Foyer, bar, auditorium all one level. Toilets. 2 spaces for wheelchair-users in the auditorium. Infra-red audio system.

Artistic Policy Polisi Artistig:

The Melville Theatre provides a focus for a whole range of theatrical and artistic activities for people in Abergavenny and the surrounding area. Regular programmes of plays, films and workshops are presented by innovative small scale professional theatre companies, with a particular focus for young people.

34 Muni Arts Centre

Gelliwastad Rd, Pontypridd CF37 2DP

Tel/Ffôn   **+44 (0) 1443 485934**
Fax/Ffacs   **+44 (0) 1443 401832**

Technical Details Manylion Technegol:

Auditorium: 12.5m x 18.5m; Stage; perf. area 6.7m x 8.12m Grid height 4.88m.
Access to the venue via dock on main road, 3.65m x 2m. Seating - 352.

Disabled resources and access Adnoddau a mynediad i'r anabl:

Loop system, disabled access to both floors, disabled toilets on both floors.

Artistic Policy Polisi Artistig:

Hire-ins, buy-ins, amateur and professional performances.

35 Theatr Mwldan

Cardigan, Ceredigion SA43 3EF

Tel/Ffôn   **+44 (0) 1239 621200**
Fax/Ffacs   **+44 (0) 1239 613600**
Email/Ebost   **boxoffice@mwldan.co.uk**
Web/Y Wê   **www.mwldan.co.uk**

Artistic Director/Cyfarwyddwr Artistig: **Dilwyn Davies**
Administrator/Gweinyddydd: **Louise O'Neill**
Technical Contact/Cyswllt Technegol:
Steven Knight theatre/theatr **William Philips** cinema/sinema

Technical Details Manylion Technegol:

Stage: 7.5m x 5.7m sprung floor, legs and masking. Seating - 159.

Disabled resources and access Adnoddau a mynediad i'r anabl:

Loop system installed, Disabled access to auditorium, café. Toilet.

Artistic Policy Polisi Artistig:

To present a diverse range of art forms to as wide a section of the community as possible.

36 Neuadd Buddug

Stryd Fawr, Y Bala

Tel/Ffôn   **+44 (0) 1678 52000**

Technical Details Manylion Technegol:

Seating - 283 (Village Hall/Neuadd y Pentre).

37 New Theatre Cardiff

Park Pl, Cardiff CF10 3LN

Tel/Ffôn   **+44 (0) 29 2087 8889** box office
              +44 (0) 29 2087 8787 admin
Fax/Ffacs   **+44 (0) 29 2087 8788**
Email/Ebost **S.A.Lewis@cardiff.gov.uk**

Administrator/Gweinyddydd: **Susan Lewis**
Technical Contact/Cyswllt Technegol: **Mark Gibbins**

Technical Details Manylion Technegol:

Pros: 9.14m wide x 6.4m high; depth of setting line 12.19m. Seating - 1156.

Disabled resources and access
Adnoddau a mynediad i'r anabl:

Level access from pavement to Box Office, Stalls Bar, adapted toilet, wheelchair positions with companion seats at the rear of the stalls; wheelchair lift to the front of the stalls; amplification system; live audio descriptions of certain performances; some performances are interpreted in British Sign Language.

Artistic Policy Polisi Artistig:

Mixed Programme Opera, Dance, Drama, Musicals, Amateur productions, Large scale Pantomime. Built 1906, this Edwardian theatre received a major refurbishment including re-modelling foyers, bars, auditorium, access on all levels. Air conditioning and restoration of the auditorium to the Edwardian character.

39 Norwegian Church Arts Centre

Harbour Dr, Cardiff Bay, Cardiff CF10 4PA

Tel/Ffôn   **+44 (0) 29 2045 4899**
Fax/Ffacs   **+44 (0) 29 2049 5122**
Email/Ebost **norwegian.church@talk21.com**

Administrator/Gweinyddydd: **Karen Allen**

Technical Details Manylion Technegol:

Auditorium: 10m x 9m; No back-stage facilities. Power points only. Seating - 100 (additional seating in upstairs gallery).

Disabled resources and access
Adnoddau a mynediad i'r anabl:

Wheelchair ramp access to ground floor only. Toilet.

Artistic Policy Polisi Artistig:

One of the most exciting arts developments in Cardiff. A small-scale venue provision and a popular draw for artists and artforms. Early music, jazz, folk, literature, contemporary music, storytelling. Encouraging local performers to promote their own concerts and striving to attract high quality touring products in early music, folk, jazz, contemporary music and literature.

38 North Wales Theatre

The Promenade, Llandudno LL30 1BB

Tel/Ffôn   **+44 (0) 1492 879771**
Fax/Ffacs   **+44 (0) 1492 860790**
Email/Ebost **nick.reed@nwtheatre.co.uk**
Web/Y Wê   **www.nwtheatre.co.uk**

Artistic Director/Cyfarwyddwr Artistig: **Nick Reed**
Technical Contact/Cyswllt Technegol: **John Owen**

Technical Details Manylion Technegol:

Largest stage in Wales: Stage width centre line to walls - SL 11.3m, SR 14.45m. Front of stage to setting line - 0.95m; Setting line to back pillars - 12.75m. Orchestra pit lift at stage level adds 2.1m fore-stage. Get-in from car park directly into scene dock - tailgate height, 3.5m high x 4.5m wide Seating 1500.

Disabled resources and access
Adnoddau a mynediad i'r anabl:

Loop system, flat access, 8 wheelchair spaces, occasional signed performances.

Artistic Policy Polisi Artistig:

Large scale receiving house: Opera, ballet, orchestral music, musical theatre, drama, comedy, variety, music.

40 Theatr y Pafiliwn

Y Promenad, Y Rhyl LL18 3AQ

Tel/Ffôn   **+44 (0) 1745 332414**
Fax/Ffacs   **+44 (0) 1745 339819**
Email/Ebost **Rhyl.pavillion@denbighshire.gov.uk**
Web/Y Wê   **www.rhylpavillion.co.uk**

Artistic Director/Cyfarwyddwr Artistig: **Gareth Owen**
Administrator/Gweinyddydd: **Val Simmons**
Technical Contact/Cyswllt Technegol: **Andrew Hughes** 01745 360088

Technical Details Manylion Technegol:

Pros: 12.9m x 6.2m, Depth to back wall 13.2m, Height to grid 16.5m Seating - 1032.

Disabled resources and access
Adnoddau a mynediad i'r anabl:

Level access to the theatre, with spaces for wheelchairs. Infra red system for hearing aid users. Toilets in foyer.

Artistic Policy Polisi Artistig:

A balanced programme of different types of art and entertainment.

41 The Pavilion

Spa Rd, Llandrindod Wells, Powys LD1 5EY

Tel/Ffôn **+44 (0) 1597 823532**
Fax/Ffacs **+44 (0) 1597 824413**
Email/Ebost **pavilion@powys.gov.uk**
Artistic Director/Cyfarwyddwr Artistig: **Carolyn Flynn**
Administrator/Gweinyddydd: **Wayne Locke**
Technical Contact/Cyswllt Technegol: **Wayne Locke**

Technical Details Manylion Technegol:

7.5 m across and 6m deep.

Disabled resources and access
Adnoddau a mynediad i'r anabl:

Access to ground floor only; Toilets.

Artistic Policy Polisi Artistig:

Mainstream Theatre, plus Ballet and small scale Opera. Seating - 565 (315 fixed in the balcony, 250 flexible seating on ground floor).

42 Park & Dare Theatre

Park & Dare Theatre, Station Rd, Treorchy, Rhondda Cynon Taff CF422 6NL

Tel/Ffôn **+44 (0) 1443 773112**
Fax/Ffacs **+44 (0) 1443 776922**

Manager/Rheolwr: **Enid Bowen**

Technical Details Manylion Technegol:

Stage: 11m wide x 6.1m deep. Seating - 700 (3) levels.

Artistic Policy Polisi Artistig:

An Edwardian proscenium-arched theatre with lounge bar, studio theatre, exhibition area, dance studio, permanent Paul Robeson Exhibition, meeting room. The Theatre acts as a venue for live performance, cinema and community events.

43 Pater Hall

Diamond St, Pembroke Dock, Pembs SA72 6DD

Tel/Ffôn **+44 (0) 1646 684410**
Fax/Ffacs **+44 (0) 1646 622788**

Artistic Director/Cyfarwyddwr Artistig: **W A Vincent**

Technical Details Manylion Technegol:

Stage: 11m wide x 6.1m deep. Seating - 255.

Artistic Policy Polisi Artistig:

Music & theatre: Lets only - local and professional use, mainly drama and music. Booking terms hire only.

44 Pontardawe Arts Centre

Herbert St, Pontardawe, Nr Swansea SA8 4ED

Tel/Ffôn **+44 (0) 1792 863722**
Fax/Ffacs **+44 (0) 1792 864137**
Email/Ebost **adickinson@npt.gov.uk**

Co-ordinator of Cultural Services/Cydlynydd Gwasanaethau Diwylliannol:
Lloyd Ellis
Acting Arts & Entertainments Manager/Rheolwr Celfyddydau Dros Dro:
Geoff Cripps
Administrator/Gweinyddydd: **Angie Dickinson**
Assistant Manager/Rheolwr Cynorthwyol: **Steve Jones**
Theatre Technician/Technegydd Theatr: **Gareth Jones**

Technical Details Manylion Technegol:

Pros: Stage; 6.7m x 8.5m perf area 5.4m high. Wing width, SL 2.4m x 3.6m, SR 3.6m x 3.6m. Wooden floor no rake, suitable for dance. Access to the venue via dock doors SL. Flexible auditorium. Seating - 425 (theatre style stalls/balcony) or reduced with cabaret seating (round tables of 8) downstairs and balcony upstairs.

Disabled resources and access
Adnoddau a mynediad i'r anabl:

Flat access directly into bar and auditorium. Toilets, induction loop, guide dogs welcome, parking.

Artistic Policy Polisi Artistig:

Arts Council supported mixed arts programme of Welsh and English language drama, music of all genres, opera, dance, literature, children's shows, exhibitions, cinema and workshops for all ages. The programme attempts to complement, rather than conflict with, neighbouring venues such as Taliesin Arts Centre in Swansea.

45 Princess Royal Theatre

Civic Centre, Port Talbot SA13 1PJ

Tel/Ffôn **+44 (0) 1639 763214**
Fax/Ffacs **+44 (0) 1639 763444**

Manager/Rheolwr: **Terry Doyle**
Technical Contact/Cyswllt Technegol: **Jonathan Davies**

Technical Details Manylion Technegol:

Pros: Stage; 13.6m (front) x 7.5m deepest point x 9.3m back wall.
Level access SL. Seating - 850 theatre style stalls/balcony. Seating reduced by using cabaret style - round tables downstairs.

Disabled resources and access Adnoddau a mynediad i'r anabl:

Parking; toilet; guide dogs welcome; induction loop; ramp access to the front of the building then flat access throughout to stalls, toilet and bar.

Artistic Policy Polisi Artistig:

Mixed programme of light entertainment including a Christmas pantomime, children's shows and performances by local amateur groups, fundraising events, dinner dances, etc.

46 St Peter's Civic Hall

Nott Square, Carmarthen SA31 1PG

Tel/Ffôn **+44 (0) 1267 235199**
Fax/Ffacs **+44 (0) 1267 221607**
Town Clerk/Clerc y Dref: **Steve Anderson**

Technical Details Manylion Technegol:

Seating - 472 (339 downstairs, 133 upstairs).

Artistic Policy Polisi Artistig:

Hired for music, dance and drama of all kinds.

47 Queens Hall

Narberth, Pembrokeshire

Tel/Ffôn **+44 (0) 1834 861212**
Email/Ebost **info@thequeenshall.com**
Web/Y Wê **www.queenshall.freeserve.co.uk**
Artistic Director/Cyfarwyddwr Artistig: **Colin Russell**

Technical Details Manylion Technegol:

5m deep x 7m wide. Seating - 200.

Disabled resources and access Adnoddau a mynediad i'r anabl:

No steps on the ground floor. Lift to all floors. Hearing loops box office and hall.

Artistic Policy Polisi Artistig:

Built in the 50s, totally refurbished in 94, the Hall is now a centre for the performing and visual arts, entertainment and business events of many kinds.

48 Rating Row

Beaumaris, Anglesey LL58 8AL

Tel/Ffôn **+44 (0) 1248 811200**
Artistic Director/Cyfarwyddwr Artistig: **Sian Mai Jones**

Technical Details Manylion Technegol:

Stage: 18m x 6m. Seating - 375.

Artistic Policy Polisi Artistig:

Music & Theatre - Orchestral Concerts, Opera Companies, Pop Concerts, Ballet, Drama, Festival Events.

49 The Royal International Pavilion

Abbey Rd, Llangollen, Denbighshire LL20 8SW

Tel/Ffôn	**+44 (0) 1978 860111**
Fax/Ffacs	**+44 (0) 1978 860046**
Email/Ebost	**enquiries@royal-pavilion.co.uk**
Web/Y Wê	**www.royal-pavilion.co.uk**

Deputy Officers/Dirprwy Swyddogion: **Carol Evans/Christine Griffith**

Technical Details Manylion Technegol:

The Hall accommodates a large screen data projection system, perfect for all multi-media. Seating - Arena - 4,500; Main Hall: 400.

Artistic Policy Polisi Artistig:

A full performance production service is available. Advice or assistance in designing seat layout, organising ticket sales, advertising, merchandising, stage-management and set design. Staff provide both technical and front of house support. The venue has full staging facilities with ample dressing room space for a full company of players. Also the versatility of our stage construction allows them to tailor the performance area to your own specific needs. Comprehensive lighting and sound control can be arranged.

50 Sherman Theatre

Senghennydd Rd, Cardiff CF24 4YE

Tel/Ffôn	**+44 (0) 29 2064 6901** admin
	+44 (0) 29 2064 6900 box office
	+44 (0) 29 2064 6909 minicom
Fax/Ffacs	**+44 (0) 29 2064 6902**
Email/Ebost	**admin@shermantheatre.demon.co.uk**

Artistic Director/Cyfarwyddwr Artistig: **Phil Clark**
General Manager/Rheolwraig Gyffredinol: **Margaret Jones**

Technical Details Manylion Technegol:

Auditorium 13.5m deep; pros 11.5m wide x 5.5m high. Seating - 468.
Arena 12m (opposite edges of gallery) x 9m deep x 6.5m wide. Full round octagon. Seating - 143-163 (flexible).

Disabled resources and access Adnoddau a mynediad i'r anabl:

Main auditorium: 2 wheelchair spaces; level access from foyer. Actors' access to main stage requires use of stairs.
Arena: Audience access via a stair lift; actor access requires use of stairs or dock door. Level access toilet facilities. Interpreted performances for the deaf, and described performances for the visually impaired are also offered on a regular basis. Free Braille and large print information.

Artistic Policy Polisi Artistig:

One of Britain's premier theatres for young people. The major producing/presenting venue in South Wales. Our mission is to create a fresh, exciting, invigorating and immediate theatre experience in an open and vital environment for young people, who are at the heart of our policy. We are committed to raising the status of theatre on the leisure agenda of young people; we aim to realise this by presenting a wide range of British and International, high quality theatre alongside Sherman Theatre Company productions at home and abroad; we celebrate our youth theatre and education activities and the work of our visiting companies. We aim to promote this unique spirit and style of theatre which will enrich the experience of all our audiences, regardless of age, our amateur and community participants and our youth theatre members. For the past 10 years, the Sherman Theatre has been at the forefront of presenting diverse and distinctive theatre for the young people of South Wales and beyond. Our resident professional Sherman Theatre Company ensures that our work is relevant, exciting and at the forefront of the arts in Wales and the UK with shows on tour throughout the country, representing Wales on a national stage. And each week our 11 Sherman Youth theatre groups provide an opportunity for over 200 young people to participate in and create their own theatre.

51 Theatr Stiwt Theatre

Stryd Lydan/Broad St, Rhosllannerchrugog,
Wrecsam LL14 1RB

Tel/Ffôn	**+44 (0) 1978 841300**
Fax/Ffacs	**+44 (0) 1978 841300**
Email/Ebost	**theatr@stiwt.co.uk**
Web/Y Wê	**www.stiwt.co.uk**

Administrator/Gweinyddydd: **David Boyce**
Technical Contact/Cyswllt Technegol: **Graham Phillips**

Technical Details Manylion Technegol:

Stage Pros: 8m x 5m Area: 15m x 12m. Seating 450-490.
Special notes Community rooms available for rehearsals, parties, full wedding licence. Exhibition area in foyer.

Disabled resources and access Adnoddau a mynediad i'r anabl:

IR (deaf/byddar). Lift and ramps to all areas other than the balcony.
Lifft neu ramp i bob rhan o'r adeilad ac eithrio'r oriel.

Artistic Policy Polisi Artistig:

Bilingual local and national for the visual arts.
Dwyieithog gymunedol a chenedlaethol i'r celfyddydau gweladwy.

Future Plans Cynlluniau at y dyfodol:

Developing the centre to encompass visual arts with an emphasis on Welsh and Welshness.
Datblygu canolfan i'r celfyddydau gweladwy gyda phwyslais ar Gymraeg a chymreictod.

52 Swansea Grand Theatre

Singleton St, Swansea SA1 3QJ

Tel/Ffôn	**+44 (0) 1792 475242** admin
	+44 (0) 1792 475715 box office
Fax/Ffacs	**+44 (0) 1792 475379**
Email/Ebost	**swansea.grand.theatre@business.ntl.com**
Web/Y Wê	**www.swanseagrand.co.uk**

General Manager/Rheolwraig Gyffredinol: **Gary Iles**
Technical Contact/Cyswllt Technegol: **Steve Miles**

Technical Details Manylion Technegol:

Auditorium Pros: 9m wide x 7m, Pros. wall to back wall 16m, Stage 29m wide, Stage to grid 22m, Stage to fly floor 9m. Bar length - 13m. 2 rehearsal areas. Non-auditorium events arranged. Dance/theatre arts school - 300 pupils. Bar/restaurant. Seating - 1026.
The Depot Studio Flexible Studio space. Seating - Up to 150.

Disabled resources and access Adnoddau a mynediad i'r anabl:

Auditorium Ground floor with ramped level access. 3 toilets. FOH. 9 wheelchair spaces. Lift to all floors. Hard of hearing induction loop system. Text phone for booking on 01792 478525.
The Depot Studio Via lift to all floors, 10 spaces available.

Artistic Policy Polisi Artistig:

Auditorium Large scale touring; opera; ballet; drama. Contemporary dance. Musical. Pantomime, children's shows plus a wide range of one-night specials.
The Depot Studio Percentage Deals, hires, buy in, other.

53 Y Tabernacl

Heol Penrallt, Machynlleth, Powys SY20 8AJ

Tel/Ffôn	**+44 (0) 1654 703355**
Fax/Ffacs	**+44 (0) 1654 702160**
Email/Ebost	**momawales@tabernac.dircon.co.uk**
Web/Y Wê	**www.tabernac.dircon.co.uk**

Administrator/Gweinyddydd: **Raymond Jones**
Technical Contact/Cyswllt Technegol: **Peter Roberts**

Technical Details Manylion Technegol:

Stage: 6.7m x 5.5m. Portable staging 6.7m x 2.7m. Ply on ironwork, suitable for dance. Get in via side doors, level access. Video projector, VCR, cinema screen, Allen organ, Steinway grand for hire. No perm tech staff, casuals available. Seating - 375.

Disabled resources and access
Adnoddau a mynediad i'r anabl:

Lift, ramped approach. 5 wheelchair spaces, assistance available. Induction loop. Backstage partially accessible to disabled performers and staff.

Artistic Policy Polisi Artistig:

To advance the aesthetic education of the public in the arts by organising, presenting and promoting exhibitions, plays, operas, films, concerts and other similar activities; and the advancement of education of the public in the study, use and appreciation of the Welsh language and culture. Y Tabernacl is a former Wesleyan chapel converted in 1986 as a centre for the performing arts. It has perfect acoustics ideal for chamber and choral music, drama, lectures and conferences. Translation booths, stage lighting, recording facilities, a sound system and a cinema screen have been installed.

54 Canolfan y Celfyddydau
Taliesin Arts Centre

University of Wales, Singleton Park, Swansea SA2 8PZ

Tel/Ffôn	**+44 (0) 1792 295238** admin
	+44 (0) 1792 296883 box office
Fax/Ffacs	**+44 (0) 1792 295889**
Email/Ebost	**s.e.crouch@swansea.ac.uk**
Web/Y Wê	**www.taliesinartcentre.co.uk**

Artistic Director/Cyfarwyddwr Artistig: **Sybil Crouch**
Technical Contact/Cyswllt Technegol: **David Palmer**

Technical Details Manylion Technegol:

Stage Flat floor adjustable pros walls. Wood floor covered in hardboard. Forestage/orchestra pit. Max. stage size 15m x 12m. Get in at rear of building stage level 2 x 6m. Seating 330/365.

Disabled resources and access
Adnoddau a mynediad i'r anabl:

Infra red and audio loop for the hearing impaired. Lift to first floor. Adapted toilet. 2 wheelchair spaces in the auditorium + 2 adapted seats. Assistance available. Carer/personal assistants free. Limited facilities for performers with disabilities.

Artistic Policy Polisi Artistig:

Broad range of programming - mainstream, innovative, physical, children's.

55 Trinity College

College Rd, Carmarthen SA31 3EP

Tel/Ffôn	**+44 (0) 1267 676767**
Email/Ebost	**tsmatk@trinity-cm.ac.uk**

Artistic Director/Cyfarwyddwr Artistig: **Marion Thomas**

Technical Details Manylion Technegol:

Halliwell Theatre: 9.5m x 6.1m. Seating - 400.
Chapel 6.1m x 6.1m. Seating - 200.
Archbishop Childs Hall 6.4m x 6.1m. Seating - 90 seats.

Artistic Policy Polisi Artistig:

Any form of music, dance or drama in the three performance areas.

56 The Torch Theatre

St Peter's Rd, Milford Haven SA73 2BU

Tel/Ffôn	**+44 (0) 1646 694192** admin
	+44 (0) 1646 695267 box office
Fax/Ffacs	**+44 (0) 1646 698919**
Email/Ebost	**info@torchtheatre.co.uk**
Web/Y Wê	**www.torchtheatre.org**

Artistic Director/Cyfarwyddwr Artistig: **Peter Doran**
Technical Contact/Cyswllt Technegol: **Davey Goffin**

Technical Details Manylion Technegol:

Stage: 10m wide pros-pros, 4.8m high, 9.6m deep excl. forestage, Floor: flat/level. Flying system: 10 x single purchase counterweights, 8 x 3 line hemp sets. Access via main foyer, stairs to auditorium. Seating - 297.

Disabled resources and access
Adnoddau a mynediad i'r anabl:

To auditorium via ramp. Lift to Bar/Toilets. Disabled toilet.

Artistic Policy Polisi Artistig:

The Torch Theatre exists to produce quality theatre and promote a mix of live theatre events that audiences find distinctive, accessible, often challenging and which stimulate interest and deepen their engagement with the performing arts.

57 Canolfan Ucheldre

Millbank, Holyhead, Anglesey LL65 1TE,

Tel/Ffôn	**+44 (0) 1407 763361**
Fax/Ffacs	**+44 (0) 1407 763341**

Artistic Director/Cyfarwyddwr Artistig: **Mike Gould**

Technical Details Manylion Technegol:

Concert Hall: Raised marble stage 6.4m x 6.4m.
Seating - Concert Hall: 180, Amphitheatre: 120 (3 tiers).

Disabled resources and access
Adnoddau a mynediad i'r anabl:

All access is level/ramped incl. gardens; Disabled toilet. Free car parking.

Artistic Policy Polisi Artistig:

This is the former chapel of a convent school which belonged to the Le Bon Sauveur order of nuns from Caen. It was taken over in 1991 by local people, extensively extended, landscaped and turned into an arts, exhibition, conference and community centre. The Centre aims to bring high quality events of all arts disciplines to Holyhead as well as encouraging local performers.

58 The Welfare

Brecon Rd, Ystradgynlais, Swansea SA9 1JJ

Tel/Ffôn	**+44 (0) 1639 843163**

Artistic Director/Cyfarwyddwr Artistig: **Wyn Roberts**
Administrator/Gweinyddydd: **Sue Aubrey**
Technical Contact/Cyswllt Technegol: **Wyn Roberts**

Technical Details Manylion Technegol:

Proscenium arch stage; 7 x 6m (10.6 x 6m to wings). Seating 300 (flexible).

Disabled resources and access
Adnoddau a mynediad i'r anabl:

Full disabled access and wheelchair spaces.

Artistic Policy Polisi Artistig:

Programmes small to mid scale theatre and dance, plus world music. Extensive community arts and education programme.

59 Welsh College of Music and Drama (wcmd)

WCMD, Castle Grounds, Cathays Park,
Cardiff CF10 3ER

Tel/Ffôn   **+44 (0) 29 2034 2854**
Fax/Ffacs   **+44 (0) 29 2039 1301**
Email/Ebost   **info@wcmd.ac.uk**
Web/Y Wê   **www.wcmd.ac.uk**

Artistic Director/Cyfarwyddwr Artistig: **Edmond Fivet**
Administrator/Gweinyddydd: **Dorothy James**
Technical Contact/Cyswllt Technegol: **Ian Evans**

Technical Details Manylion Technegol:

British Steel Recital Room* Light, airy room, high ceiling. Grand piano. Polished wooden floor. Suitable for meetings. Green room nearby. Seating 50.
Bute Theatre* Space 12m x 10m. Good height clearance. Get-in direct to stage. Concrete floor. Full lighting rig/sound facilities. Seating - 168 (bench 64).
Caird Studio Space max 8m x 11m. Get-in 3rd floor, passenger lift access. Height restriction 4m. Hardwood floor. Limited lighting rig/sound facilities. Seating - up to 50.
Sir Geraint Evans Recital Room* Raised carpeted stage 8m x 4m, separate lighting/curtains. Yamaha Concert grand piano. Linked to Recording Studio Dressing area. Seating - 50.
S4C Studio* Space 10m x 6m, high ceiling. Ground floor, reasonable access. Hardwood floor covered black vinyl. Recording Studio. Seating - 50.
Weston Gallery* Light, airy room with high ceiling. Steinway grand piano. Polished wooden floor. Recording Studio. Suitable for meetings. Green room nearby. Seating - 80.
* Very limited availability due to heavy student use

Disabled resources and access Adnoddau a mynediad i'r anabl:

Weston Gallery 4 wheelchair spaces, Hearing induction loop. Guide dogs welcome
Bute Theatre 4 wheelchair spaces, Hearing induction loop. Guide dogs welcome
Caird Studio 2 wheelchair spaces, access lift. Hearing induction loop. Guide dogs welcome
Sir Geraint Evans Recital Room
3 wheelchair spaces, access lift. Hearing induction loop. Guide dogs welcome
S4C Studio 2 wheelchair spaces, Hearing induction loop. Guide dogs welcome.
Weston Gallery 4 wheelchair spaces, Hearing induction loop. Guide dogs welcome

Artistic Policy Polisi Artistig:

To provide performance-centred and practically based courses which enable students to enter and influence the music and theatre professions and their related industries and, being aware of its unique position as the major provider of this type of education in Wales, to fulfil its responsibilities and develop its role in a European and international framework.

60 Wyeside Arts Centre / Canolfan Glan Gwy

Castle St, Builth Wells, Powys LD2 3BN

Tel/Ffôn   **+44 (0) 1982 553668**
Fax/Ffacs   **+44 (0) 1982 553995**
Email/Ebost   **box@wyeside.co.uk**
Web/Y Wê   **www.wyeside.co.uk**

Artistic Director/Cyfarwyddwr Artistig: **Guy Roderick**
Administrator/Gweinyddydd: **Debbie Burch**
Technical Contact/Cyswllt Technegol: **Chris Sennett**

Technical Details Manylion Technegol:

Stage: 10m wide x 7.5m deep. Height to grid 6m. Open 7 days a week. Youth dance/theatre workshops. Seating - Auditorium 249 (max) Cinema 200.

Disabled resources and access Adnoddau a mynediad i'r anabl:

Infra red hearing facilities. Toilet. Lift to all floors.

Artistic Policy Polisi Artistig:

Broad based regional venue with separate cinema and gallery. Community based creative initiatives and workshops.

FESTIVALS
GWYLIAU

[1] Abergavenny Festival / Gŵyl y Fenni

c/o Abergavenny Information, The Swan Meadows, Cross St, Abergavenny NP75HH
Tel/Ffôn +44 (0) 1873 857588
Fax/Ffacs +44 (0) 1873 850217
Email/Ebost abergavenny-tic@monmouthshire.gov.uk
July-August: A packed programme of music, drama, literature, folk, jazz, choirs, children's events, workshops and art exhibitions.

[2] Gŵyl Caernarfon Festival

3 Stryd y Plas, Caernarfon, Gwynedd LL55 1RR
Tel/Ffôn +44 (0) 1286 678800
Fax/Ffacs +44 (0) 1286 672201
Email/Ebost caernarfon.festival@btinternet.com
July-August: A varied festival to suit all ages set in the historic town of Caernarfon, including circus and performing arts workshops and music and theatre in the evenings.

[3] Cambria Arts Easter Festival / Gŵyl Gelfyddydau Cambria

Tregaron, Bridgend, Llanddewi Brefi, Tregaron, Ceredigion
Tel/Ffôn +44 (0) 1974 298719
Fax/Ffacs +44 (0) 1974 298719
Email/Ebost cambriaarts@btinternet.com
March-May: A varied arts festival including visual arts, craft fair, concerts, film, puppet theatre and workshops.

[4] The Dylan Thomas Celebration / Dylan Thomas: Y Dathliad

Dylan Thomas Centre, Somerset Pl, Abertawe SA1 1RR
Tel/Ffôn +44 (0) 1792 463980
Fax/Ffacs +44 (0) 1792 463993
Email/Ebost dylanthomas@cableol.co.uk
Web/Y Wê www.dylanthomas.org
October-November: Celebration of the life and work of Dylan Thomas and others in words, music and pictures.

[5] National Eisteddfod of Wales / Eisteddfod Genedlaethol Cymru

40 Parc Ty Glas, Llanishen, Cardiff CF14 5WU
Tel/Ffôn +44 (0) 29 2076 3777
Fax/Ffacs +44 (0) 29 2076 3737
Email/Ebost info@eisteddfod.org.uk
Web/Y Wê www.eisteddfod.org.uk
August: Wales's largest arts festival celebrating over 800 years of tradition, a unique festival to Wales.

[6] Eisteddfod Genedlaethol Urdd Gobaith Cymru

Swyddfa'r Urdd, Ffordd Llanbadarn, Aberystwyth SY23 1EN
Tel/Ffôn +44 (0) 1970 613100
Fax/Ffacs +44 (0) 1970 626120
Email/Ebost aber@urdd.org
Web/Y Wê www.urdd.org
May-June: Europe's largest youth festival.

[7] Gŵyl Fawr Aberteifi

Teifi Leisure Centre Cardigan, Des Davies, Min Y Maes, Penparc
Cardigan, Ceredigion SA43 1RE
Tel/Ffôn   +44 (0) 1239 615914
Email/Ebost des_davies@lineone.net
June-July: Concerts,competitions, music, folk singing and dance.

[8] Gŵyl Ystalyfera

Swyddfa Gŵyl Ystalyfera, 80 Commercial St
Ystalyfera, Swansea SA9 2HS
Tel/Ffôn   +44 (0) 1639 841225
Email/Ebost gwyl@ystalyfera.org
Web/Y Wê www.ystalyfera.org
July: Three day music festival, festival procession and children's entertainment.

[9] Llandrindod Wells Victorian Festival / Gŵyl Fictorianaidd Llandrindod Wells

Festival Office, Temple St, Llandrindod Wells, Powys LD1 5DL
Tel/Ffôn   +44 (0) 1597 823441
Fax/Ffacs +44 (0) 1597 825905
Email/Ebost info@victorianfestival.co.uk
Web/Y Wê www.victorianfestival.co.uk
August: A 9 day festival providing a full range of family entertainment. The
varied programme provides events including workshops, exhibitions, talks,
concerts and variety shows, plus street theatre performances.

[10] Llanw Llyfrau / Booktide Children's Arts Festival

Nest Powys Davies, Activities Librarian, Ceredigion Library,
Corporation St, Aberystwyth SY23 2BU
Tel/Ffôn   +44 (0) 1970 633702
Email/Ebost nestd@ceredigion.gov.uk
October-November: Annual festival for children focussing on literature with a
programme of performances, readings, workshops and other events taking place
at three venues in Ceredigion: Aberystwyth Arts Centre, Theatr Felinfach, Theatr
Mwldan, Cardigan.

[11] Pontardawe International Music Festival / Gŵyl Gerddoriaeth Ryngwladol Pontardawe

Festival Office, Pontardawe Inn, Pontardawe, Swansea SA8 4UD
Tel/Ffôn   +44 (0) 1792 830200
Fax/Ffacs +44 (0) 1792 930649
Email/Ebost pontardawe.festival@eclipse.co.uk
Web/Y Wê www.pontardawefestival.org.uk
August: 24 years of music and dance, folk, world and rock in three outdoor
arenas.

Practitioners

Y M A R F E R W Y R

Choreographers
COREOGRAFFWYR

June Campbell-Davies
4 Brunel St, Riverside, Cardiff CF1 8ES
Tel/Ffôn   +44 (0) 29 2022 2067
Specialism/Arbenigaeth: **Freelance dancer, choreographer**

Douglas Comley
22 Bridle Mews, Limeslade, Mumbles
Swansea SA3 4JP
Tel/Ffôn   +44 (0) 1792 361380
+44 (0) 7811 784090 mobile
Specialism/Arbenigaeth: **Freelance choreographer**

Ruth Douglas
32 Heol Penrallt, Machynlleth, Powys SY20 8AJ
Tel/Ffôn   +44 (0) 7762 738068
Specialism/Arbenigaeth: **Freelance choreographer**

Sean Tuan John
15 Rookwood St, Grangetown,
Cardiff CF11 6PH
Tel/Ffôn   +44 (0) 7712 208998
+44 (0) 29 2025 7518
Specialism/Arbenigaeth: **Innovative dance work; national and international touring**
Selected pieces/darnau dethol: Frederick's First Kiss; Poor White Trash; Dances for Aliens (with Bert van Gorp)

Jurg Koch
75 Kings Rd, Cardiff CF11 9DB
Tel/Ffôn   +44 (0) 029 2065 1544
+44 (0) 7967 559639 mobile
Email/Ebost jurgkoch@ntlworld.com
Specialism/Arbenigaeth: **Freelance dancer, teacher, choreographer**

Eddie Ladd
26 Moira Pl, Adamsdown, Cardiff CF24 0ET
Tel/Ffôn   +44 (0) 7974 394415 mobile
Email/Ebost eddie@dybli.fsnet.co.uk
Specialism/Arbenigaeth: **Creates, tours Welsh work**
Selected pieces/darnau dethol: Llath, Scarface

Caroline Lamb
116 Kimberly Rd, Penylan, Cardiff CF2 5DN
Tel/Ffôn   +44 (0) 29 2049 5079
Specialism/Arbenigaeth: **Freelance choreographer**

Belinda Neave
67 Richards Ter, Roath, Cardiff CF24 1RW
Tel/Ffôn   +44 (0) 29 2031 2434
Specialism/Arbenigaeth: **Freelance choreographer**

Paul Anthony O'Brien
4 Mount View, Top Rd, Summerhill, Wrexham
Tel/Ffôn   +44 (0) 1978 756976
+44 (0) 7751 077617 mobile
Specialism/Arbenigaeth: **Freelance choreographer**

Denise Powling
12c Singleton Rd, Splott, Cardiff CF24 2ES
Tel/Ffôn   +44 (0) 29 2047 0663
+44 (0) 7977 203373 mobile
Specialism/Arbenigaeth: **Freelance choreographer**

Jo Shapland
Rosehaven, Allt Fach, St Dogmaels,
Pembrokeshire SA43 3HA
Tel-Fax/Ffôn-Ffacs +44 (0) 1239 613148
+44 (0) 7813 199136 mobile
Email/Ebost joshapland@yahoo.co.uk
Specialism/Arbenigaeth: **freelance dance-theatre, voice, multi-disciplinary performance**
Selected pieces/darnau dethol: Zeitlupe; Pedestal; Soluna, See the Woods through the Trees.

Ian Spink
The Old School House, Dernol, Llangurig,
Powys SY16 6RZ
Tel/Ffôn   +44 (0) 1686 440658
Fax/Ffacs   +44 (0) 1686 440315
Email/Ebost zspink@netscapeonline.co.uk
Specialism/Arbenigaeth: **Director, choreographer, Australian Ballet, Richard Alston, Scottish Opera, Welsh National Opera, Second Stride. Black Dogs**
Selected pieces/darnau dethol: Les Troyans;Tannhauser; The Tempest

Jem Treays
11 Ovington Ter, Llandaff, Cardiff CF5 1GF
Tel/Ffôn   +44 (0) 29 2064 5905
Email/Ebost treaysj@wcmd.ac.uk
Specialism/Arbenigaeth: **Choreographer; Movement director**
Selected pieces/darnau dethol: Wall; Walkie Talkie; Faust, Hamlet (for NYTW)

Anushiye Yarnell
18 University Pl, Splott, Cardiff
Tel/Ffôn   +44 (0) 29 2031 1237
Specialism/Arbenigaeth: **Freelance choreographer**

Designers
CYNLLUNWYR

Simon Banham
Glyn Peris, Llanon, Ceredigion SY23 5HJ
Tel/Ffôn   +44 (0) 1974 202240
+44 (0) 7967 810543 mobile
Email/Ebost shb@aber.ac.uk
Specialism/Arbenigaeth: **Freelance stage designer, former head of design at Contact Theatre Manchester, now at Aberystwyth University. Over 20 professional productions throughout Europe, South America and India.**
Selected plays/Dramâu dethol: Nokan Kyem Til a Komme; See-Saw; Punch & Judy

Lucy Bevan
The Old School House, Dernol, Llangurig,
Powys SY18 6RZ
Tel/Ffôn   +44 (0) 1686 440658
Fax/Ffacs   +44 (0) 1686 440315
Email/Ebost spinkbevan@btinternet.com
Specialism/Arbenigaeth: **Freelance set & costume designer, .**
Selected plays/Dramâu dethol: The Soldier's Tale; Cosi Fan Tuttie; The Glass Menagerie

Beth Maldive Davies
30 Coldra Rd, Newport, S Wales NP20 4FF
Tel/Ffôn   +44 (0) 1633 215550
+44 (0) 7799 228899 mobile
Specialism/Arbenigaeth: **Set & Costume design for Theatre, Opera, Film & TV**
Selected plays/Dramâu dethol: The Importance of Being Earnest, Down In The Valley, Faust

Steve Denton
30 Coldra Rd, Newport, S Wales NP20 4FF
Tel/Ffôn   +44 (0) 1633 215550
+44 (0) 7867 873307
Specialism/Arbenigaeth: **Set & Costume design for Theatre, Dance & Film**
Selected plays/Dramâu dethol: Jane Eyre, Generations, Crossing The Parallels

Elizabeth Fenwick

Cwrt, Penrhyncoch, Aberystwyth SY23 3EG
Tel/Ffôn   +44 (0) 1970 820157
Specialism/Arbenigaeth: **Freelance designer
working primarily in theatre through the
mediums of Welsh and English.**
Selected plays/Dramâu dethol: Dilema, Lab'l, All's Fair

Steve Mattison

Caecarrog, Aberhosan, Machynlleth
Tel/Ffôn   +44 (0) 1654 703247
Email/Ebost **steve@carrog.co.uk**
Web/Wê   **www.carrog.co.uk**
Specialism/Arbenigaeth: **Freelance set designer.**
Selected plays/Dramâu dethol: Ty Ni, Yn ein Dwylo, Caliesin, Y Ffin, Another Country, One Moonlit Night

Martin Morley

8 Frondeg, Bethesda, Gwynedd LL57 3SW
Tel/Ffôn   +44 (0) 1248 601315
          +44 (0) 7770 877956 mobile
Email/Ebost **morleymartin@hotmail.com**
Specialism/Arbenigaeth: **Freelance stage designer**
Selected plays/Dramâu dethol: Amadeus; O Law i law; Pwy sy'n sal

Meri Wells

Caecarrog, Aberhosan, Machynlleth
Tel/Ffôn   +44 (0) 1654 703247
Email/Ebost **meri@carrog.co.uk**
Web/Wê   **www.carrog.co.uk**
Specialism/Arbenigaeth: **Freelance stage
designer; works in English and Welsh**
Selected plays/Dramâu dethol: Regan; Diwrnod Branwen; Mis Bach Ddu/Black February

Carolyn Willitts

33 Lansdaune Rd, Canton, Cardiff
Email/Ebost **carolyn.willitts@net.ntl.com**
Specialism/Arbenigaeth: **Freelance designer**
Selected plays/Dramâu dethol: Front Steps; Queen of Hearts; Gulp

Directors
CYFARWYDDWYR

Tim Baker

29 Hendy Rd, Mold, Flintshire CH7 1QS
Tel/Ffôn   +44 (0) 1352 758857
          +44 (0) 7977 555203 mobile
Email/Ebost **baker.eames@virgin.net**
Specialism/Arbenigaeth: **Director, Adapting,
Welsh/English - Cyfarwyddwr, Cyfaddasu,
Cymraeg/Saesneg**
Selected plays/Dramâu dethol: Accidental Death of an Anarchist, Hard Times, Flora's war, Of Mice And Men, The Cordell Trilogy, To Kill a Mockingbird, Celf

Stuart H Bawler

Shining Wits Productions, 5 Laundry Pl,
Abergavenny NP7 5DN
Tel/Ffôn   +44 (0) 1873 858090
Email/Ebost **schnibob@aol.com**
Specialism/Arbenigaeth: **U.V. Comedy**
Selected plays/Dramâu dethol: Jason and the golden fleas, Dragons at Dinas Emrys

Richard Cheshire

Ty Melin, Cwm Rheidol, Aberystwyth,
Ceredigion SY23 3NB
Tel/Ffôn   +44 (0) 1970 880776
          +44 (0) 7818 066187 mobile
Fax/Ffacs   +44 (0) 1970 622831
Email/Ebost **rac@aber.ac.uk**
Specialism/Arbenigaeth: **Freelance director,
classical texts, pantomime, musicals.**
Selected plays/Dramâu dethol: The Way of the World, Teechers, Glass Menagerie, Salad Days, Me and My Girl, Puss In Boots, Aladdin

Phil Clark

Sherman Theatre, Senghenydd Rd,
Cardiff CF24 4YE
Tel/Ffôn   +44 (0) 29 2064 6901
Fax/Ffacs   +44 (0) 29 2064 692
Specialism/Arbenigaeth: **Artistic Director, New
Writing, Devising, Freelance**
Selected plays/Dramâu dethol: Flesh&Blood, The Mad Millennium, Crackers Xmas, Everything must go, Unprotected sex, Oyster Catchers

Stephen Fisher

c/o Sherman Theatre, Senghenydd Rd,
Cathays, Cardiff CF24 4YE
Tel/Ffôn   +44 (0) 29 2064 6901
          +44 (0) 7970 422505
Fax/Ffacs   +44 (0) 29 2064 6900
Email/Ebost **sfisher@
          shermantheatre.demon.co.uk**
Specialism/Arbenigaeth: **Directing - Theatre,
Television, Radio, Physical Theatre**
Selected plays/Dramâu dethol: Saturday Night Forever, Gas station angel, N.A.T.H.A.N, Con-tract

Richard Gough

c/o CPR 6 Science Park, Aberystwyth SY23 3AH
Tel/Ffôn   +44 (0) 1970 622133
Web/Y Wê   **rig@aber.ac.uk**
Specialism/Arbenigaeth: **Devised Theatre - Food,
Cookery**
Selected plays/Dramâu dethol: The Origin of Table Manners, The Burning of the Dancers, From Honey to Ashes, Brasil, The Black Dinner, Amsterdam, The Last Supper

Jill Greenhalgh

Bodwenog, Llangrannog, Llandysul SA44 6SQ
Tel/Ffôn   +44 (0) 1239 654136
Fax/Ffacs   +44 (0) 1239 654136
Email/Ebost **jill.greenhalgh@talk21.com**
Web/Y Wê   **www.themagdalenaproject.com**
Specialism/Arbenigaeth: **International Director
and Producer, Artistic Director of the
Magdalena Project International Network of
Women in Contemporary Theatre**
Selected projects/Prosiectau dethol: The Bl/reeding Ground, Magdalena Aotearoa, Magdalena Festival of Voice, Raw Visions, Midnight Level 6, Child, Magdalena Pacifica 2002, The Water[war]s, 7 Attempted Crossings of the Straits of Gibraltar

Richard Hand

Dept Of Theatre And Media Drama, University
Of Glamorgan, Pontypridd CF37 1DL
Tel/Ffôn   +44 (0) 1443 480480
Fax/Ffacs   +44 (0) 1443 482138
Email/Ebost **rhand@glam.ac.uk**
Web/Y Wê   **www.glam.ac.uk**
Specialism/Arbenigaeth: **Director, Writer, Adapting
fiction into theatre, History in drama, Grand -
Guignol**
Selected plays/Dramâu dethol: Dakota, Laughing Anne, Where the Road Leads, Leopard 223

Terry Hands
c/o Clwyd Theatre Cymru, Mold, Flintshire,
North Wales CH7 1YA
Tel/Ffôn   +44 (0) 1352 756331
Fax/Ffacs   +44 (0) 1352 755177
Email/Ebost **drama@celtic.co.uk**
Web/Y Wê **www.clwyd-theatr-cymru.co.uk**
Specialism/Arbenigaeth: **Director - Theatre, Opera**

Simon Harris
c/o The Rod Hall Agency, 7 The Goodge Pl,
London W1P 1FL
Tel/Ffôn   +44 (0) 20 7637 0706
Fax/Ffacs   +44 (0) 20 7637 0807
Email/Ebost **office@rodhallagency.com**
Web/Y Wê **www.rodhallagency.co.uk**
Specialism/Arbenigaeth: **Playwright, Director,
Associate Director Sgript Cymru/Contemporary
Drama Wales**
Selected plays/Dramâu dethol: Valley Girl, Mog's Rock,
Badfinger, Wales>Alaska, Garageland, Forever Yours
Marie Lou, Nothing To Pay

Martin Houghton
c/o Welsh College of Music and Drama, Castle
grounds, Cathays Park, Cardiff CF1 3ER
Tel/Ffôn   +44 (0) 7811 854460
Email/Ebost **martin.houghton@ntlword.com**
Specialism/Arbenigaeth: **Director - Theatre, TIE,
Touring, Rep Theatre**

Derec Jones
43 Maes Rd, Llangennech, Llanelli SA14 8UH
Tel/Ffôn   +44 (0) 1554 820473
Email/Ebost **derec@budsoft.com**
Web/Y Wê **www.derec.freeserve.co.uk**
Specialism/Arbenigaeth: **Artistic Director**
Selected plays/Dramâu dethol: The History of
Llangennech - Part 2

Steve Allan Jones
22 Derwen Drive, Rhyl, North Wales LL18 2PB
Tel/Ffôn   +44 (0) 1745 351520
    +44 (0) 7971 517642
Email/Ebost **stevesaj@aol.com**
Specialism/Arbenigaeth: **Musical Director,
Composer**
Selected plays/Dramâu dethol: Blah, Blah, Blah, Alice
In Wonderland, Toad of Toad Hall, The Nativity, Alice
Through The Looking Glass, Adrian Mole, Little Shop of
Horrors

Euros Lewis
Alma, Cribyn, Dyffryn Aeron,
Ceredigion SA48 7ND
Tel/Ffôn   +44 (0) 1570 470135
Fax/Ffacs   +44 (0) 1570 471030
Email/Ebost **euros@theatrfelinfach.demon.co.uk**
Web/Y Wê **www.theatrfelinfach.demon.co.uk**
Specialism/Arbenigaeth: **Writer/Director - Youth/
Community Theatre, Pantomimes / Ysgrifennu,
Cyfarwyddo cwmniau ieuenctud a theatr
gymunedol**
Selected plays/Dramâu dethol: Pantomimes

Kevin Lewis
31 Llandaff Rd, Canton, Cardiff CF11 9NG
Tel/Ffôn   +44 (0) 29 2022 6945
Email/Ebost **s.argent@tesco.net**
Specialism/Arbenigaeth: **Director - Intercultural,
Youth Theatre, Maskwork, Puppetry,
Storytelling**
Selected plays/Dramâu dethol: Bison and sons, By a
thread, Stars, The Flood, The Sleepwalker, Marcos, The
Tempest

John Lovat
2 Stanhope St, Abergavenny, Gwent NP7 7DH
Tel/Ffôn   +44 (0) 1873 851622
Email/Ebost **jqc@btinternet.com**
Specialism/Arbenigaeth: **Youth Theatre Director**
Selected plays/Dramâu dethol: Starstone, Fall,
Confusions, Grimm's Fairy Tales, The Barber of Savile Row,
Pinnocchio, Cinderella, Kalafs Quest, Phantasia

Robin Phillips
Ty Coch, Village Rd, Maeshafn, Mold,
Flintshire CH7 5LR
Tel/Ffôn   +44 (0) 1352 810467
Email/Ebost **robin@vocals.co.uk**
Specialism/Arbenigaeth: **Director, Adapting
Children's fiction, Youth theatre,
Student/School Workshops**
Selected plays/Dramâu dethol: Blood Brothers, Cherry
Orchard, A Midsummer Night's Dream, Teechers, Hayfever,
Murder In The Cathedral

Menna Price
Via Savio 38, Ravenna, Italy RA 48100
Tel/Ffôn   +39 (0) 5446 6595 Ravenna
    +44 (0) 29 2025 8922 Cardiff
Email/Ebost **mennaprice@libero.it**
Specialism/Arbenigaeth: **Self-employed director/
Cyfarwyddydd Theatr Hunan-gyflogedig**
Selected plays/Dramâu dethol: The Caretaker's plot,
IFOR 2000, The Threepenny Opera, Mystery Bouffe, Animc
Farm, A Slag's Gig

David Ian Rabey
Gwynfryn, Newtown Rd, Machynlleth,
Powys SY20 8EY
Tel/Ffôn   +44 (0) 1654 702200
Email/Ebost **davidian@rabey.fsbusiness.co.uk**
Specialism/Arbenigaeth: **New Expressionist
Productions, Radical Reassessments of
Contemporary Drama**
Selected plays/Dramâu dethol: The Battle of Crows, Bit
or Suck, The Back of Beyond, Skin Shanty, Uncle Vanya,
That Slidey Dark

Ian Rowlands
c/o Bill McLean, 23b Deodar Rd, Putney,
Llundain SW15 2NP
Tel/Ffôn   +44 (0) 20 8789 8191
Fax/Ffacs   +44 (0) 20 8789 8191
Email/Ebost **ianrowlands@appleonline.net**
Specialism/Arbenigaeth: **Artistic Director, Writer -
TV, Theatre/Cyfarwyddwr Artistig, Awdur -
Teledu, Theatr**
Selected plays/Dramâu dethol: Mor Tawel, 00, Pacific,
Marriage of convenience, Blue Heron in the womb, New
South Wales

Andrew Sterry
c/o Ashleigh, Dyffryn Rd, Llandrindod Wells,
Powys LD16 AN
Tel/Ffôn   +44 (0) 1597 824672
Email/Ebost **itsaonkey@hotmail.com**
Specialism/Arbenigaeth: **Director**
Selected plays/Dramâu dethol: Cinderella, The Comedy
Of Errors, Life's a dream, Wind!, Everything must go, Flesh
and blood, The Twits, East From The Gantry, Nobody here
but us chickens

David Hedley Williams
Minnis Pitts, Cresselly, Cilgeti,
Sir Benfro SA68 OSJ
Tel/Ffôn **+44 (0) 1646 651264**
Fax/Ffacs **+44 (0) 1646 651264**
Specialism/Arbenigaeth: **Bilingual Writer,**
Director/Sgriptiwr, Cyfarwyddwr dwyieithog
Selected plays/Dramâu dethol: Imbed! Imbed!, Y
Calendr, Ghosts for a summer knight, Gan Bwyll

Sêra Moore Williams
Tel/Ffôn **+44 (0) 1970 625347**
Fax/Ffacs **+44 (0) 1970 625347**
Email/Ebost **Gymraes@appleonline.net**
Specialism/Arbenigaeth: **Director**
Selected plays/Dramâu dethol: Ffair, Gormod o
Ddim, Haearn, Mor Forwyn

James Tyson
Tel/Ffôn **+44 (0) 29 2031 1054**
Specialism/Arbenigaeth: **Independent theatre**
maker, Director
Selected plays/Dramâu dethol: Woyzeck, The End of
Theatre (or love songs for the 21st century)

Phillip Zarrilli
Tyn-y-parc, Ceredigion SA47 0PB
Email/Ebost **p.zarrilli@exeter.ac.uk**
Specialism/Arbenigaeth: **Director, Training**
performers through Martial Arts
Selected plays/Dramâu dethol: The Beckett Project Ohio
Impromptu, Not I, Act Without Words, Rockaby, Was?
Wer? Ohio Impromptu, Spiel, Eh Joe

Writers
AWDURON

Stuart Allen
10 Church Rd, Llansamlet, Swansea SA7 9RH
Tel/Ffôn **+44 (0) 1792 414470**
    +44 (0) 2087 405016
Email/Ebost **kingofthejungle99@yahoo.com**
Specialism/Arbenigaeth: **Playwright**
Selected plays/Dramâu dethol: King of the jungle

Sarah Argent
31 Llandaff Rd, Canton, Cardiff CF11 9NG
Tel/Ffôn **+44 (0) 29 2022 6945**
Email/Ebost **s.argent@tesco.net**
Specialism/Arbenigaeth: **Writer, Translator, Youth**
Theatre
Selected plays/Dramâu dethol: Born Bad, Maze of
power, Wimp!, Henry and the Seahorse

Lewis Davies
53, Colum Rd,Cardiff
Tel/Ffôn **+44 (0) 29 2034 1314**
Fax/Ffacs **+44 (0) 29 2034 1314**
Email/Ebost **parthianbooks@yahoo.co.uk**
Web/Y Wê **www.parthianbooks.co.uk**
Selected plays/Dramâu dethol: My Piece of Happiness
(1998); Without Leave (1998)

Richard Downing
Rock Cottage, Llanbadarn Fawr, Aberystwyth,
Ceredigion SY23 3SG
Tel/Ffôn **+44 (0) 1970 626764**
Fax/Ffacs **+44 (0) 1970 622831**
Email/Ebost **mail@umanzoo.org**
Web/Y Wê **www.umanzoo.org**
Specialism/Arbenigaeth: **Writer, director,**
scenographer. Adopts an holistic approach to
the making of performance as extraordinary
encounter in unorthodox places.
Selected plays/Dramâu dethol: Motorcity, Dome, Kite,
32 Wardrobes

Margie Douglas
20 The Village, Clyro, Powys, Hereford HR3 5SF
Tel/Ffôn **+44 (0) 1497 821061**
Email/Ebost **p.m.j.brett@care4free.net**
Specialism/Arbenigaeth: **Writer/Director,**
Community, youth, dance & musical theatre
Selected plays/Dramâu dethol: Ladder to the moon,
Red Kite, Karaoke Night, Picture In The Sand, Hours by the
window

Dic Edwards
MLR, Douglas House, Douglas St,
Westminster, SW1P 4PB /
8 Greenland Terrace, Aberaeron,
Ceredigion SA46 OER
Tel/Ffôn **+44 (0) 1545 571265**
Email/Ebost **dicedwards@**
    playwright30.freeserve.co.uk
Web/Y Wê **www.playwright30.**
    freeserve.co.uk
Specialism/Arbenigaeth: **Playwright**
Selected plays/Dramâu dethol: Over Milk Wood, The
Man Who Gave His Foot For Love, Kid, Vertigo, The
freewheelers, Lola Brecht, Casanova Undone,
Wittgenstein's Daughter, The Beggars New Clothes

Glyndwr Edwards
10 Twynbedw, Cymmer, Porth,
Rhondda Cynon Taff CF39 9HR
Tel/Ffôn **+44 (0) 7967 235055**
Specialism/Arbenigaeth: **Writer, Welsh folklore**
Selected plays/Dramâu dethol: The Oldest Animals,
Endless Night, The changeling, Summer's almost gone,
Sleep easy, Mother of all sailors

Sion Eirian
19 Boverton St, Cardiff CF23 5ES
Email/Ebost **sioneirian@genie.co.uk**
Specialism/Arbenigaeth: **Bilingual Writer**
Selected plays/Dramâu dethol: Cegin y Diafol, Paradwys
Waed, Sibrwd yn y Nos, Epa yn y Parlwr Cefn, Woman of
Flowers

Huw Emlyn
Llysawel, 4 Heol Y Graig, Aberaeron,
Ceredigion SA46 0JP
Tel/Ffôn **+44 (0) 1545 570967**
Fax/Ffacs **+44 (0) 1545 570967**
Email/Ebost **huwcyn@aol.com**
Specialism/Arbenigaeth: **Musicals, community**
groups/Dramau Cerdd, Grwpiau Cymunedol
Selected plays/Dramâu dethol: Mab Y Mynydd, Cor Bro
Dysynni, Dryswch y drysau, Gwelyau'n iawn, Iechyd Da

Lucy Gough
Bronheulog, Fronfraith Lane, Comins Coch,
Aberystwyth, Ceredigion SY23 3BE
Tel/Ffôn   +44 (0) 1970 625580
Fax/Ffacs   +44 (0) 1970 627987
Email/Ebost **Lucy.Gough@care4free.net**
Web/Y Wê   **www.Lucy.Gough.care4free.net**
Specialism/Arbenigaeth: **Playwright-for Theatre,
TV and Radio; Radio Drama Lecturer**
Selected plays/Dramâu dethol: Sheol, Mapping the
Soul, Wolfskin, Rushes, Stars, Haul, Crossing the Bar, As to
be Naked (Is the Best Disguise), Our Lady of Shadows, By
a Thread, Catherine Wheel

Gareth Ioan
Croesheddig Newydd, Pentre'r Bryn, Y Synod,
Llandysul, Ceredigion
Tel/Ffôn   +44 (0) 1545 560255
Fax/Ffacs   +44 (0) 1545 560255
Email/Ebost **xheddig@aol.com**
Specialism/Arbenigaeth: **Youth and community
theatre, musicals/Theatr ieuenctud a
chymuned, Sioeau cerdd Cymanfa ganu**
Selected plays/Dramâu dethol: Mab y Mynydd, Adar
2000, Syrffio ar sgwar, Dal dy dir

Mark Jenkins
12 Eider Close, Cardiff CF3 ODF
Tel/Ffôn   +44(0) 29 2030 0955
Fax/Ffacs   +44 (0) 29 2030 0955
Email/Ebost **mark.jenkins12@ntlworld.com**
Specialism/Arbenigaeth: **Playwright**
Selected plays/Dramâu dethol: Birthmarks, Downtown
Paradise, Mr.Owen's Millennium, Playing Burton,
Strindberg Knew my Father

Patrick Jones
8 Falcon Terrace, Brynawel,
Crosskeys NP11 7QY
Tel/Ffôn   +44 (0) 1495 271194
Email/Ebost **patrickjones@lineone.com**
Web/Y Wê   **www.patrickjones.co.uk**
Specialism/Arbenigaeth: **Poet/Playwright**
Selected plays/Dramâu dethol: Everything Must Go,
Unprotected Sex

Geraint Lewis
11 The Parade, Yr Eglwys Newydd,
Cardiff CF14 2EE
Tel/Ffôn   +44 (0) 29 2040 0316
Email/Ebost **lewisparade@ntlworld.com**
Specialism/Arbenigaeth: **Comedy scriptwriter/
Awdur comedi**
Selected plays/Dramâu dethol: Ysbryd Beca, Y cinio,
Meindiwch eich busnes, Y groesffordd, The language of
heaven

Stephanie Marshall
Bryn Seion Chapel, Heol-y-graig, Aberporth,
Ceredigion SA43 2HB
Tel/Ffôn   +44 (0) 1239 810866
Email/Ebost **dramaticimprovement@
          btinternet.com**
Specialism/Arbenigaeth: **Writer/Producer, St
Theatre, Pantomime, Adapting, Filming
Theatre, Performance Art**
Selected plays/Dramâu dethol: The Dream Show

Philip Michell
19 Walters St, Manselton, Swansea SA5 9PL
Tel/Ffôn   +44 (0) 1792 424882
Email/Ebost **philip.michell@ntlworld.com**
Specialism/Arbenigaeth: **Playwright - Film,
Theatre, Television**
Selected plays/Dramâu dethol: Dance of the Dragon,
The Reincarnations of Elizabeth R, Skylark Song, Words,
Words, Words!, Homefront, A Room Of My Own, Knights In
The City

Gareth Miles
26 Graigwen Parc, Pontypridd CF37 2ST
Tel/Ffôn   +44 (0) 1443 485106
Fax/Ffacs   +44 (0) 01443 485106
Specialism/Arbenigaeth: **Dramatist, scriptwriter,
translator (French, Spanish, English)**
Selected plays/Dramâu dethol: Diwedd y Saithdegau,
Duges Amalffi, Y Bacchai, Hunllef yng Nghymru Fydd,
Calon Ci, Y Madogwys.

Alan Osborne
123 West Lee, Cowbridge Rd East, Canton,
Cardiff CF11 9DT
Tel/Ffôn   +44 (0) 29 2030 4718
Specialism/Arbenigaeth: **Writer, Librettist, Director**
Selected plays/Dramâu dethol: Katya Katerina,
Precious, Redemption Song, The Beach Inspector, Lapo &
Lodo, Retrospective

Wynford Ellis Owen
10 Queen Charlotte Dr, Creigiau,
Cardiff CF15 9NY
Tel/Ffôn   +44 (0) 29 2089 2323
Fax/Ffacs   +44 (0) 29 2089 1811
Email/Ebost **wynfordowen@aol.com**
Specialism/Arbenigaeth: **Writer - Welsh Film,
Television, Radio, Theatre**
Selected plays/Dramâu dethol: Gwin Goch a Fodca, Por
Peis Bach, Yv Aelod

Kaite O'Reilly
c/o Sebastian Born, The Agency, 24 Pottery
Lane, Holland Park, London
Specialism/Arbenigaeth: **Writing - Theatre, Radio**
Selected plays/Dramâu dethol: The Hen House, YARD,
Belonging, Commissions

Meic Povey
35 Plasturton Gdns, Pontcanna,
Cardiff CF11 9HG
Tel/Ffôn   +44 (0) 29 2023 1901
Email/Ebost **meicpovey@aol.com**
Specialism/Arbenigaeth: **Playwright/Awdur**
Selected plays/Dramâu dethol: Tair, Wyneb yn Wyneb,
Yn Debyg iawn i ti a fi, Perthyn

Neil Rhodes
Well Cottage, Wern, Llanymynech SY22 6PF
Tel/Ffôn   +44 (0) 1691 831249
Fax/Ffacs   +44 (0) 8701 323831
Email/Ebost **nrhodes1@ntlworld.com**
Specialism/Arbenigaeth: **Playwright**
Selected plays/Dramâu dethol: Killing time, Frank
exchange, Gearknobs and dipsticks

Adrian Ross
21 Pinewood Close, Malpas Park, Newport,
Gwent NP20 6WR
Tel/Ffôn   +44 (0) 1633 790096
Email/Ebost **arts.development@
          newport.gov.uk**
Specialism/Arbenigaeth: **Studio Theatre, Place
and Time, Nationality, Self-identity**
Selected plays/Dramâu dethol: The Miracle Of Mendozo

Ian Rowlands
c/o Bill McLean, 23b Deodar St,
Putney, Llundain
Tel/Ffôn   +44 (0) 20 8789 8191
Fax/Ffacs   +44 (0) 20 8789 8191
Email/Ebost   ianrowlands@appleonline.net
Specialism/Arbenigrwydd: **Artistic director, writer tv,
theatre/ Cyfarwyddwr Artistig, Awdur Teledu a
theatr**
Selected plays/Dramâu dethol: Mor Tawel, Pacific, Marriage
of convenience, Blue Heron in the womb, New South Wales

Othniel Smith
2a Maplewood Flats, Maplewood Ave,
Cardiff CF14 2NA
Tel/Ffôn   +44 (0) 7710 797396
Email/Ebost   othnielsmith@yahoo.com
Web/Y Wê   www.geosites.com/othniel_s/
Specialism/Arbenigaeth: **Playwright - Radio,
Theatre**
Selected plays/Dramâu dethol: D.M.S.R, Giant Steps,
Singing The O'Riley Song

Tracy Spotiswoode
65 Oakfield St, Roath, Cardiff CF24 3RF
Tel/Ffôn   +44 (0) 29 2049 3827
Fax/Ffacs   +44 (0) 29 2049 3827
Email/Ebost   Living-Doll@msn.com
Specialism/Arbenigaeth: **Writer, Animator, Actor,
Czech speaker**
Selected plays/Dramâu dethol: Voice, Taffia, The
Observatory, Ablutions, Dare, Islands, Za Zrcadlem through
the looking glass

Christine Watkins
57 Redlands Rd, Penarth CF64 2WE
Tel/Ffôn   +44 (0) 1981 540509
Fax/Ffacs   +44 (0) 1981 540509
Email/Ebost   christine.watkins@virgin.net
Web/Y Wê   www.welcome-velkommen.com
Specialism/Arbenigaeth: **Writing - Theatre, Film
Ysgrifennu - Theatr, Film**
Selected plays/Dramâu dethol: Welcome to my world,
Rosa, Hocuspocus, Queen Of Hearts, The Sea that blazed,
Black Febuary/Mis Bach Du, The Biker King

Ieuan Watkins
7, Pen-Y-Coed, Nannerch, Mold,
Flintshire CH7 5RS
Tel/Ffôn   +44 (0) 1352 741818
Specialism/Arbenigaeth: **Writer**
Selected plays/Dramâu dethol: Facing Up

Charles Way
49 St Helen's Rd, Abergavenny, Gwent NP7 5YA
Tel/Ffôn   +44 (0) 1873 858559
Email/Ebost   charles.way@btinternet.com
Specialism/Arbenigaeth: **Freelance Writer**
Selected plays/Dramâu dethol: She Scored for Wales, In
the Bleak Midwinter, Paradise Drive, Ill Met By Moonlight,
The Dove Maiden, On the Black Hill, The Search for
Odysseus, A spell of Cold Weather, Playing from the heart,
Sleeping Beauty, The Night Before Christmas, Somebody
Loves You, Beauty and the Beast, Red Red Shoes, The
Flood, Dead man's hat, One snowy night.

David Hedley Williams
Minnis Pitts, Cresselly, Cilgeti, Sir Benfro, SA68
0SJ
Tel/Ffôn   +44 (0) 1646 651264
Fax/Ffacs   +44 (0) 1646 651264
Specialism/Arbenigrwydd: **Bilingual - Writer,
director. Sgriptiwr, Cyfarwyddwr dwyieithog**
Selected plays/Dramâu dethol: Imbed! Imbed!, Y
Calendr, Ghosts for a summer knight, Gan Bwyll

Aled Jones Williams
Y Ficerdy, Ffordd Penamser, Porthmadog,
Gwynedd LL49 9PA
Tel/Ffôn   +44 (0) 1766 514951
Fax/Ffacs   +44 (0) 1766 514951
Email/Ebost   marbeth@globalnet.co.uk
Specialism/Arbenigaeth: **Scriptwriter / Awdur
drama**
Selected plays/Dramâu dethol: Tiwlips, Wal, Cnawd, Pel
Goch, Sundance

Roger Williams
7 Heol Danlan, Penbre, Porth Tywyn,
Sir Gaerfyrddin SA16 0UF
Tel/Ffôn   +44 (0) 1554 834579
Email/Ebost   rogerwilliams@msn.com
Specialism/Arbenigaeth: **Bilingual playwright -
Theatre, TV, Radio/Dramodydd dwyieithog -
Theatr, Deledu, Radio**
Selected plays/Dramâu dethol: Pop, Killing Kangaroos,
Calon Lan, Gulp, Love in Aberdare, Saturday night forever,
Surfing, Carmarthen Bay

Sêra Moore Williams
Tel/Ffôn   +44 (0) 1970 625347
Fax/Ffacs   +44 (0) 1970 625347
Email/Ebost   Gymraes@appleonline.net
Specialism/Arbenigaeth: **Playwright**
Selected plays/Dramâu dethol: Byth Rhy Hwyr/Never
Too late, Yn y Gorlan/ In the Fold, Mefus/
Strawberries, Rownd y Byd Mewn Lori/Around The
World in a Lorry, Mab/Son

Resources

ADNODDAU

SUPPORT ORGANISATIONS SEFYDLIADAU CEFNOGI

Arts Care-Gofal Celf ltd
St Davids Hospital, Jobswell Rd, Carmarthen,
Carmarthenshire, SA31 3HB
Tel/Ffôn   +44 (0) 1267 223341
Fax/Ffacs   +44 (0) 1267 223403
Email/Ebost   info@acgc93.freeserve.co.uk
Organisation which specialises in the placing of
professional artists in all artforms into health and
social care contexts, mainly in West Wales.

The Arts Council of Wales – Cyngor Celfyddydau Cymru
9 Museum Pl, Cardiff CF10 3NX
Tel/Ffôn   +44 (0) 29 2037 6500
Fax/Ffacs   +44 (0) 29 2022 1477
Email/Ebost   information@cc-acw.org.uk
Web/Y Wê   www.ccc-acw.org
Aims to achieve an even spread of opportunities for
participation, to develop and improve knowledge and
understanding of the arts in Wales. Main source of
funds, an annual grant from the National Assembly
and the National Lottery. From these the ACW offers
annual revenue and project funding to arts
organisations. New and pilot funding schemes come
into operation on a regular basis detailed in ACW's
'A Guide to grants from the Arts Council of Wales' or
by consulting the ACW website.

**Wales Arts International –
Celfyddydau Rhyngwladol Cymru**
A joint initiative between the ACW and the British
Council in Wales to encourage collaborative projects in
Wales with producers, presenters and artists from
abroad. There are two schemes : Inter-link and Inter-
recce. Contact the International Department of ACW or:
Web/Y Wê   www.wai.org.uk
Night Out
An ACW scheme that helps local organisations to bring
professional performances into community buildings at
subsidised prices. Contact ACW:
Web/Y Wê   www.nightout.org.uk

Arts Disability Wales – Anabledd Celfydddydau Cymru
Sbectrwm, The Old School, Bwlch Rd, Fairwater,
Cardiff CF5 3EF
Tel/Ffôn   +44 (0) 7971 480154
Email/Ebost   arts.disability@wales.com
Web/Y Wê   www.artsdisability.com
Advice, training and information.

CADMAD
Boston Buildings, 70 James St,
Cardiff CF10 5EZ
Tel/Ffôn   +44 (0) 29 2045 2808
Fax/Ffacs   +44 (0) 29 2045 2809
Email/Ebost   info@cadmadltd.
freeserve.co.uk
A multicultural agency developing and promoting the
arts of diverse minority ethnic groups in Wales. Runs
programmes which raise awareness and understanding
of cultural diversity.

Centre for Performance Research
6 The Science Park, Aberystwyth SY23 3AH
Tel/Ffôn   +44 (0) 1970 622133
Fax/Ffacs   +44 (0) 1970 622132
Email/Ebost   cprwww@aber.ac.uk
Web/Wê   www.thecpr.org.uk
Pioneering theatre organisation with the following
aims: to develop and improve the knowledge,
understanding and practice of theatre through research
and sharing; to focus on contemporary practice;
innovation and experimentation and the relationship to
theatre tradition; the integration of theory and practice,
extending boundaries, perception and possibilities. The
CPR holds conferences, summer schools, festivals and
exchanges and produces tours of international
performances. They also document and publish
material on performance and are an international
resource for research and information.

Y Cylch / the Circuit
Red House, Bettws, Newtown, Powys SY16 3LE
Tel/Ffôn   +44 (0) 1686 610554
Fax/Ffacs   +44 (0) 1686 610554

Community Dance Wales – Dawns Cymunedol Cymru
Sbectrwm, Bwlch Rd, Fairwater, Cardiff CF5 3EF
Tel/Ffôn   +44 (0) 29 2057 5075
Fax/Ffacs   +44 (0) 29 2057 5073
Email/Ebost   info@communitydancewales
.com
Web/Y Wê   www.communitydancewales
.com
Umbrella and development body with emphasis on
access and participation. Provides advocacy, training,
information and advice to raise the profile of
community dance in Wales.

Creu Cymru
Asiantaethteithio i Gymru /
Touring Agency for Wales
8H, Parc Gwyddoniaeth/Science Park,
Llanbadarn Fawr, Aberystwyth SY23 3AH
Tel/Ffôn   +44 (0) 1970 639444
Email/Ebost   post@creucymru.co.uk
Web/Y Wê   www.creucymru.co.uk
Develops and co-ordinates the provision of
performing arts touring; provides audience
development projects to its membership of
professionally run venues in Wales.

Cultural Enterprise Menter Diwyllianol
Chapter, Heol y Farchnad, Caerdydd CF5 1QE
Tel/Ffôn   +44 (0) 29 2034 3205
Fax/Ffacs   +44 (0) 29 2034 5436
Email/Ebost   mail@cultural-enterprise.com
Web/Y Wê   www.cultural-enterprise.com
Free information and advice for cultural industries'
practitioners and small companies.
*Gybodaeth a chyngor yn rhad ac am ddim i ymarferwyr a
chwmniau bychain yn y diwydiannau diwylliannol.*

The Drama Association of Wales – Cymdeithas Drama Cymru
The Old Library, Singleton Rd, Splott, Cardiff CF24 2ET
Tel/Ffôn +44 (0) 29 2045 2200
Fax/Ffacs +44 (0) 29 2045 2277
Email/Ebost aled.daw@virgin.net
Web/Y Wê www.amdram.co.uk
The Drama Association of Wales is the umbrella body for amateur theatre in Wales - offering; support, advice, training and services including play publishing and a play library, throughout the Principality and beyond.
Mae Cymdeithas Ddrama Cymru yn gorff sydd wedi ymrwymo i hyrwyddo, i gefnogi ac i gynnig arweiniad a gwasanaethau amrywiol megis llyfrgell ddrama a chyhoeddi dramâu, i fudiad y ddrama amatur yng Nghymru a thu hwnt.

Equity
Wales & South West Office, Transport House, 1 Cathedral Rd, Cardiff CF11 9SD
Tel/Ffôn +44 (0) 29 2039 7971
Fax/Ffacs +44 (0) 29 2023 0754
Email/Ebost cryde@cardiff-equity.org.uk
Web/Y Wê www.equity.org.uk
Represents the professional interests of performers and artists across the entire spectrum of entertainment and the arts. Those interests include negotiating minimum wages, terms and conditions; providing help and advice; legal protection; job information and insurance cover.

Festivals of Wales
PO Box 20, Conwy LL32 8ZQ
Tel/Ffôn +44 (0) 1492 573760
Fax/Ffacs +44 (0) 1492 573760
Email/Ebost kay@festivalsof wales. freeserve.co.uk

Independent Theatre Council
12 The Leathermarket, Weston St, London SE1 3ER
Tel/Ffôn +44 (0) 20 7403 1727
Fax/Ffacs +44 (0) 20 7403 1745
Email/Ebost admin@itc-arts.org
Web/Y Wê www.itc-arts.org
Advisory service to members and training provider.

Wales ITI Cymru
University of Glamorgan, Pontypridd CF37 1DL
Tel/Ffôn +44 (0) 1443 483346
Email/Ebost iti@glam.ac.uk
The Wales Centre of the International Theatre Institute / UNESCO. Funded in 2002 by the National Assembly of Wales to raise the profile of Welsh theatre nationally and internationally. walesITIcymru does this with an ongoing programme to retrieve, record and make accessible the history, development and practice of performance in Wales, and also initiates international-exchange projects etc with various partners. Bilingual and prioritises the involvement of young people.

National Assembly for Wales – Cynulliad Cenedlaethol Cymru
Cardiff Bay, Cardiff CF99 1NA
Tel/Ffôn +44 (0) 29 2089 8200
Fax/Ffacs +44 (0) 29 2089 8229
Email/Ebost Assembly.Info@wales. gsi.gov.uk
Web/Y Wê www.wales.gov.uk

National Youth Theatre of Wales – Theatr Ieuenctid Cenedlaethol Cymru
WJEC, 245 Western Ave, Cardiff CF5 2YX
Tel/Ffôn +44 (0) 29 2026 5006
Fax/Ffacs +44 (0) 29 2026 5014
Email/Ebost nytw@nyaw.co.uk
Web/Y Wê www.nyaw.co.uk/nytw
Provides artistically challenging theatre experiences which enhance and extend youth theatre opportunities available locally.

Permanent Waves – Cymdeithas Celfyddydau Menywod
Recreate, Wroughton Pl, Ely Bridge, Cardiff CF5 4AB
Tel/Ffôn +44 (0) 29 2056 9800 (fax/ffacs)
Email/Ebost pw@recreate.demon.co.uk
Web/Y Wê www.recreate.demon.co.uk www.1000dreams.co.uk
A women's arts association; organises projects, network, conference and festivals, mainly SE Wales.

Voluntary Arts Wales – Celfyddydau Gwirfoddol Gymru
PO Box 200, Welshpool, Powys SY21 7WN
Tel/Ffôn +44 (0) 1938 556455
Fax/Ffacs +44 (0) 1938 556451
Email/Ebost info@vaw.org.uk
Web/Y Wê www.voluntaryarts.org
Supports participation in the arts by working with national and regional voluntary arts organisations, local authorities and policy makers and funders. Provides information, advice and training.

Wales Association for the Performing Arts (WAPA) – Cymdeithas Celfyddydau Perfformio Cymru
WAPA, PO Box 443, Cardiff CF11 9YT
Tel/Ffôn +44 (0) 29 2057 5075
Email/Ebost waparts@hotmail.com
Web/Y Wê www.waparts.co.uk
The principal umbrella organisation for the professional performing arts in Wales. Membership is open to all non profit distributing companies as well as interested individuals. The association provides information and training, organises general meetings and seminars, and campaigns and lobbies extensively on behalf of the professional sector.
Corff ambarel ar gyfer cwmniau celfyddydau performio porffesiynol yng Nghymru, yn cynrychioli theatr, opera a dawns.

Cymdeithas Ddawns Werin Cymru – Welsh Folk Dance Society
Ffynonnlwyd, Trelech, Carmarthen SA33 6QZ
Tel/ Ffon   +44 (0) 1994 484496
Email/Ebost   dafydde@welshfolkdance.org.uk
bobtob@ic24.net

Welsh Independent Dance
Chapter, Market Rd, Canton, Cardiff CF5 1QE
Tel/Ffôn   +44 (0) 29 2038 7314
Email/Ebost   welshindance@freenet.co.uk
An artist led umbrella organisation for independent dancers and choreographers living and working in Wales. Supports and nurtures practitioners; organises touring productions and community residencies.

Writers' Guild of Great Britain (Wales)
Room 23, 13 Market St, Pontypridd CF37 2ST

Undeb yr Ysgrifenwyr
13 Heol y Farchnad, Pontypridd CF37 2EQ
Tel/Ffôn   +44 (0) 1443 485106
Fax/Ffacs   +44 (0) 1443 485106
The trade union for professional writers. Affiliated to the TUC and TUC Wales. Represents writers for theatre, TV, film, radio and publishing.
Yr undeb llafur ar gyfer awduron proffesiynol. Aelod o'r TUC a TUC Cymru. Yn cynrychioli awduron theatr, teledu, ffilm a llên.

Regional Community Dance Organisations
Blackwood Miners' Institute High St, Blackwood NP12 1BB
Tel/Ffôn   +44 (0) 1495 227206
Fax/Ffacs   +44 (0) 1495 226457

Dance Blast Chepstow Library, Manor Way, Chepstow Monmouthshire NP16 5HZ
Tel/Ffôn   +44 (0) 1291 635631 (fax/ffacs)
Email/Ebost   emmacarlson@madasafish.com
emmacarlsonwales@hotmail.com

Dawns Dyfed Theatr Felinfach, Llanbedr Pont Steffan, Ceredigion
Tel/Ffôn   +44 (0) 1570 471049 (fax/ffacs)
Email/Ebost   rheoli@dawnsdyfed.co.uk
mags@dawnsdyfed.co.uk

Dawns i Bawb 117 High St, Porthmadog, Gwynedd LL49 9HA
Tel/Ffôn   +44 (0) 1766 515243
Fax/Ffacs   +44 (0) 1766 515244
Email/Ebost   dawns-i-bawb@lineone.com

Dawns Powys Dance
The Dance Centre, Arlais Rd, Llandrindod Wells, Powys LD1 5HE
Tel/Ffôn   +44 (0) 1597 824370 (fax/ffacs)
Email/Ebost   powys.dance@powys.gov.uk

Dawns TAN Dance Baglan Community Centre, Hawthorn Ave, Baglan, Neath, Port Talbot SA12 8PG
Tel/Ffôn   +44 (0) 1639 813428
Fax/Ffacs   +44 (0) 1639 823487
Email/Ebost   tan.dance@virgin.net

NE Wales Dance Yale College, Grove Pk Rd, Wrexham LL12 7AA
Tel/Ffôn   +44 (0) 1978 316447
Fax/Ffacs   +44 (0) 1978 291569
Email/Ebost   newcd@yale.ac.uk

Rhondda Cynon Taf Community Arts
Park & Dare Theatre, Station Rd, Treorchy, Rhondda Cynon Taf CF42 6NL
Tel/Ffôn   +44 (0) 1443 776090
Fax/Ffacs   +44 (0) 1443 776922
Email/Ebost   enquiry@communityarts-rhonddacynontaf.co.uk

Rubicon Dance Nora St, Adamsdown, Cardiff CF24 1ND
Tel/Ffôn   +44 (0) 29 2049 1477
Fax/Facs   +44 (0) 29 2047 2240
Email/Ebost   info@rubicondance.co.uk
Web/Y Wê   www.rubicondance.co.uk

LOCAL AUTHORITY ARTS OFFICERS SWYDDOGION Y CELFYDDYDAU AWDURODAU LLEOL

Welsh Local Government Association
Local Government House, Drake Walk, Cardiff CF10 4LG
Chris Llewelyn Head of Education, Training and Cultural Affairs
Tel/Ffôn   +44 (0) 29 2046 8614
Fax/Ffacs   +44 (0) 29 2046 8601
Email/Ebost   wlga@wlga.gov.uk
Web/Y Wê   www.wlga.gov.uk

Blaenau Gwent County Borough Council
Richard Hughes
Tel/Ffôn   +44 (0) 1495 308996

Bridgend County Borough Council
Roger Price
Tel/Ffôn   +44 (0) 1656 642684

Caerphilly County Borough Council
Kate Strudwick
Tel/Ffôn   +44 (0) 1495 224425
+44 (0) 1443 815588

Cardiff County Council
Glenda Charles
Tel/Ffôn   +44 (0) 29 2087 8513

Carmarthenshire County Council
Phillip Alder
Tel/Ffôn   +44 (0) 1267 224834

Ceredigion County Council
Geraint Lewis
Tel/Ffôn   +44 (0) 1970 633700

Conwy County Borough Council

Ann Williams
Tel/Ffôn   +44 (0) 1492 575371

Denbighshire County Council

Steve Brake
Tel/Ffôn   +44 (0) 1824 708210

Flintshire County Council

Margaret Evans
Tel/Ffôn   +44 (0) 1352 704105

Gwynedd County Council

Ann Rowena
Tel/Ffôn   +44 (0) 1758 704086

Isle of Anglesey County Council

Alan Griffiths
Tel/Ffôn   +44 (0) 1248 752024

Merthyr Tydfil County Borough Council

Kuth Taylor Davies
Tel/Ffôn   +44 (0) 1685 725143

Monmouthshire County Council

Peter Ellis
Tel/Ffôn   +44 (0) 1633 644644

Neath Port Talbot County Borough Council

Marlene Adams
Tel/Ffôn   +44 (0) 1639 763149

Newport County Borough Council

Chris Smith
Tel/Ffôn   +44 (0) 1633 244491

Pembrokeshire County Council

Mel Lucking
Tel/Ffôn   +44 (0) 1437 764551

Powys County Council

Louise Ingham
Tel/Ffôn   +44 (0) 1597 826000

Rhondda Cynon Taff County Borough Council

Louise Carey
Tel/Ffôn   +44 (0) 1443 409526

Swansea City & County

Robin Hall
Tel/Ffôn   +44 (0) 1792 651738

Torfaen County Borough Council

Christine Willison
Tel/Ffôn   +44 (0) 1495 762200

Vale of Glamorgan Council

Tracey Harding
Tel/Ffôn   +44 (0) 1446 700111

Wrexham County Borough Council

Tracey Simpson
Tel/Ffôn   +44 (0) 1978 292093

FUNDING OPPORTUNITIES FFYNONELLAU ARIANNOL

Arts & Business Cymru – Celfyddyd & Busnes Cymru

16 Museum Pl, Cardiff CF10 3BH
Tel/Ffôn   +44 (0) 29 2030 3023
Fax/Ffacs   +44 (0) 29 2030 3024
Email/Ebost   cymru@AandB.org.uk
Web/Y Wê   www.aandb.org.uk
Room 5, 1-2 Chapel St, Llandudno LL30 2SY
Tel/Ffôn   +44 (0) 1492 574003
Email/Ebost lorraine.hopkins@AandB.org.uk
Encourages partnerships between business and the arts. Services include sponsorship seminars, free advice sessions, an arts networking forum and training and mentoring programmes for business and arts managers. The New Partners programme can provide cash investments in partnerships between a business and arts organisation / artist.

The Arts Council of Wales – Cyngor Celfyddydau Cymru

Holst House, 9 Museum Pl, Cardiff CF10 3NX
Tel/Ffôn   +44 (0) 29 2037 6500
Fax/Ffacs   +44 (0) 29 2022 1477
Email/Ebost   information@cc-acw.org.uk
Web/Y Wê   www.ccc-acw.org
Aims to achieve an even spread of opportunities for participation, to develop and improve knowledge and understanding of the arts in Wales. Main source of funds, an annual grant from the National Assembly and the National Lottery. From these the ACW offers annual revenue and project funding to arts organisations. New and pilot funding schemes come into operation on a regular basis detailed in ACW's 'A Guide to grants from the Arts Council of Wales' or by consulting the ACW website.

The British Council Wales
28 Park Pl, Cardiff CF10 3QE
Tel/Ffôn   +44 (0) 29 2039 7346
Fax/Ffacs   +44 (0) 29 2023 7494
Email/Ebost tony.deyes@britishcouncil.org
Web/Y Wê   www.britishcouncil.org
Advice and sometimes financial assistance for high quality theatre and dance activity overseas.

Directory of Social Change
24 Stephenson Way, London NW1 2DP
Tel/Ffôn   +44 (0) 20 7209 5151
Fax/Ffacs   +44 (0) 20 7209 4804
Web/Y Wê   www.dsc.org.uk
Low cost publications and training about fundraising (including an Arts Funding Guide) and about voluntary sector management, communication, finance and law.

Welsh European Funding Office WEFO – Swyddfa Cyllid Ewropeaidd Cymru
Wales/European Programme Executive, The Old Primary School, Machynlleth SY20 8PE
Tel/Ffôn   +44 (0) 1654 704900
Fax/Ffacs   +44 (0) 1654 704909
Funds available from ESF for specific types of project in specific areas of Wales, subject to meeting the criteria.

Foundation for Sports and the Arts – Sefydliad ar gyfer Chwaraeon a'r Celfyddydau
PO Box 20, Liverpool LI3 1HB
Tel/Ffôn   +44 (0) 151 259 5505
Fax/Ffacs   +44 (0) 151 230 0664
Awards to help enhance the use of existing facilities and to assist with established projects eg events, festivals, productions. Also assists with revenue funding in short/medium terms.

National Lotteries Charities Board – Bwrdd Elusennau'r Loteri Genedlaethol
Wales Office, Ladywell House, Newtown, Powys SY16 1JB
Tel/Ffôn   +44 (0) 1686 611700
Fax/Ffacs   +44 (0) 1686 621534
Email/Ebost enquires.wales@community-fund.org.uk
Access to small grants - between £500 and £5000; or larger grants under Poverty and Disadvantage and Community Involvement programmes. For charitable organisations with an annual income of less than £15,000 proposing projects which include community involvement.

New Opportunities Fund – Y Gronfa Cyfleoedd Newydd
13th Floor Capital Tower, Greyfriars Rd, Cardiff CF10 3AG
Tel/Ffôn   +44 (0) 29 2067 8200
Fax/Ffacs   +44 (0) 29 2066 7275
Email/Ebost peter.bryant@nof.org.uk
Web/Y Wê   www.nof.org.uk
Funding derived from the National Lottery for health, education and environmental schemes to be managed by local consortia of organisations and partnerships of different kinds.

The Welsh Language Board WLB – Bwrdd yr Iaith Gymraeg
Market Chambers, 5-7 St Mary St, Cardiff CF10 1AT
Tel/Ffôn   +44 (0) 29 2022 4744
The WLB offers grants to assist with developing your Welsh language scheme eg producing publicity material.

EDUCATION & TRAINING ADDYSG A HYFFORDDIANT
HIGHER EDUCATION
ADDYSG UWCH

University of Wales Aberystwyth
Admissions, Old College, King St, Aberystwyth SY23 2AX
Tel/Ffôn   +44 (0) 1970 622021
Email/Ebost ug-admissions@aber.ac.uk
Web/Y Wê   www.aber.ac.uk
Drama   BA Hons.
Drama/Performing Arts BA Hons joint degree with a wide range of subjects
Drama   MA

University of Wales Bangor
Bangor, Gwynedd LL57 2DG
Tel/Ffôn   +44 (0) 1248 382017
Email/Ebost Admissions@bangor.ac.uk
Web/Y Wê   www.bangor.ac.uk
Drama   BA Hons in the 'Arts Group'
English with Theatre Studies
Cymraeg ac Theatr a'r Cyfryngau
Astudiaethau Theatr a'r Cyfryngau.

University of Wales Institute Cardiff
PO Box 377, Llandaff Campus, Western Ave, Cardiff CF5 2SG
Tel/Ffôn   +44 (0) 29 2041 6070
Web/Y Wê   www.uwic.ac.uk
Drama   BA/BA Hons with QTS, Secondary Education

University of Glamorgan
Treforest, Pontypridd CF37 1DL
Tel/Ffôn   +44 (0) 1443 480480
Email/Ebost   enquiries@glam.ac.uk
Web/Y Wê   www.glam.ac.uk
Theatre & Media Drama BA/BA Hons, in joint and combined degrees.
Theatre Studies HND (at Bridgend College of Technology campus)

Llandrillo College
Llandudno Rd, Colwyn Bay LL28 4HZ
Tel/Ffôn   +44 (0) 1492 542338
Email/Ebost   admissions@llandrillo.ac.uk
Web/Y Wê   www.llandrillo.ac.uk
Community Theatre
HND/HNC (approval: 2001/02)

Swansea Institute of Higher Education
Town Hill Campus, Town Hill Rd, Swansea SA2 0UT
Tel/Ffôn   +44 (0) 1792 481000
Web/Y Wê   www.sihe.ac.uk
Theatre Studies BA Hons with various subjects

Trinity College, Carmarthen
College Rd, Carmarthen SA31 3EP
Tel/Ffôn   +44 (0) 1267 676767
Email/Ebost   k.matherick@trinity-cm.ac.uk
Web/Y Wê   www.trinity-cm.ac.uk
Theatre Studies, Theatre Design & Production BA Hons;
Theatre Studies, Movement in Performance & Theatre Studies
BA Hons joint degrees with various subjects (approval: 2001/02)

Welsh College of Music & Drama
Castle Grounds, Cathays Park, Cardiff CF10 3ER
Tel/Ffôn   +44 (0) 29 2034 2854
Web/Y Wê   www.wcmd.ac.uk
Acting, Stage Management, Theatre Design BA Hons
Post-graduate diplomas

Bridgend College
Cowbridge Rd, Bridgend Mid Glam CF31 3DF
Tel/Ffôn   +44 (0) 1656 302302
Email/Ebost   admissions@bridgend.ac.uk
Web/Y Wê   www.bridgend.ac.uk
Performing Arts Certificate **P**
First Diploma **F**
National Diploma **F**

Coleg Sir Gâr (CCTA)
Graig Campus, Sandy Rd, Llanelli SA15 4DN
Tel/Ffôn   +44 (0) 1554 748000
Email/Ebost   admissions@colegsirgar.ac.uk
Web/Y Wê   www.colegsirgar.ac.uk
Performing Arts National Diploma **F**

Coleg Ceredigion, Llanbadarn
Llanbadarn Fawr, Aberystwyth SY23 3BP
Tel/Ffôn   +44 (0) 1970 624511
Web/Y Wê   www.ceredigion.ac.uk
Performing Arts (Acting / Contemporary Dance / Technical Skills)   National Diploma **F**

Coleg Glan Hafren
Trowbridge Rd, Rumney, Cardiff CF3 8XZ
Tel/Ffôn   +44 (0) 29 2025 0250
Email/Ebost   enquiries@glan-hafren.ac.uk
Web/Y Wê   www.glan-hafren.ac.uk
Media & Performing Arts
Intermediate Diploma **F**
Performing Arts National Diploma **F**

Gorseinon College
Belgrave Rd, Gorseinon, Swansea SA4 6RD
Tel/Ffôn   +44 (0) 1792 890700
Email/Ebost   admin@gorseinon.ac.uk
Web/Y Wê   www.gorseinon.ac.uk
Performing Arts National Diploma **F**

Coleg Gwent
Email/Ebost   info@coleggwent.ac.uk
Web/Y Wê   www.coleggwent.ac.uk

Crosskeys
Risca Rd, Crosskeys, Gwent NP11 7ZA
Tel/Ffôn   +44 (0) 1495 333456
Dance National Diploma **F**
Drama National Diploma **F**
Performing Arts First Diploma **F**
Theatre & Media (Make-Up / Hairdressing / Wigmaking) Diploma **F**
Theatre & Media (Make-Up) Diploma **E**

Ebbw Vale
College Rd, Ebbw Vale, Gwent NP23 6GT
Tel/Ffôn   +44 (0) 1495 333000
Performing Arts (Rock & Pop) First Diploma **F**
National Diploma **F**

Newport
Nash Rd, Newport, Gwent NP19 4TS
Tel/Ffôn   +44 (0) 1633 466000
Music Technology/Sound Engineering NOCN Advanced Diploma **F**

Llandrillo College
Llandudno Rd, Rhos-on-Sea, Colwyn Bay, Clwyd LL28 4HZ
Tel/Ffôn   +44 (0) 1492 546666
Email/Ebost   a.bettley@llandrillo.ac.uk
Web/Y Wê   www.llandrillo.ac.uk
Performing Arts First Diploma **F**
National Diploma **F**
HND **F**
Theatrical & Media (Make-Up) Diploma **E**

Coleg Meirion-Dwyfor
Penrallt, Pwllheli, Gwynedd LL53 5UB
Tel/Ffôn   **+44 (0) 1758 701385**
Web/Y Wê   **www.meirion-dwyfor.ac.uk**
Performing Arts National Diploma **F**

Coleg Menai
Llangefni, Gwynedd LL57 2TP
Tel/Ffôn   **+44 (0) 1248 370125**
Email/Ebost   **student.services@
menai.ac.uk**
Web/Y Wê   **www.menai.ac.uk**
Performing Arts First Diploma **F**
National Diploma **F**

Merthyr Tydfil College
Ynysfach, Merthyr Tydfil, Mid Glam CF48 1AR
Tel/Ffôn   **+44 (0) 1685 726000**
Email/Ebost   **college@merthyr.ac.uk**
Web/Y Wê   **www.merthyr.ac.uk**
Performing Arts First Diploma **F**
National Diploma **F**

Pembrokeshire College
Haverfordwest, Pembrokeshire SA61 1SZ
Tel/Ffôn   **+44 (0) 1437 765247**
Email/Ebost   **info@pembrokeshire.ac.uk**
Web/Y Wê   **www.pembrokeshire.ac.uk**
Performing Arts First Diploma **F** & **D**
Drama/Technical Theatre National Diploma **F**

Pontypridd College
Ynys Terr, Rhydyfelin, Pontypridd,
Mid Glam CF37 5RN
Tel/Ffôn   **+44 (0) 1443 662800**
Email/Ebost   **college@pontypridd.ac.uk**
Web/Y Wê   **www.pontypridd.ac.uk**
Performing Arts First Diploma **F**
National Diploma **F**
**Theatrical Media Make-up / Creative
Hair Design** Certificate **F**
Music Technology National Diploma **F**

Coleg Powys
Llanidloes Rd, Newtown, Powys SY16 4HU
Tel/Ffôn   **+44 (0) 1686 622722**
Email/Ebost   **enquiries@coleg-powys.ac.uk**
Web/Y Wê   **www.coleg-powys.ac.uk**
Performing Arts National Diploma **F**

Swansea College
Tycoch, Swansea SA2 9EB
Tel/Ffôn   **+44 (0) 1792 284000**
Web/Y Wê   **www.swancoll.ac.uk**
Performing Arts National Diploma **F**

University of Wales Swansea
Dept of Continuing Education,
Adult Continuing Education
University of Wales Swansea SA2 8PP
Informal and Accredited Courses; Cert. HE Community
Arts Practice

Welsh College of Music & Drama
Castle Grounds, Cathays Park, Cardiff CF1 3ER
Tel/Ffôn   **+44 (0) 29 2034 2845**
Email/Ebost   **info@wcmd.ac.uk**
Web/Y Wê   **www.wcmd.ac.uk**
Acting Advanced Diploma **F**
Stage Management
Advanced Diploma **F**

Yale College
Grove Park Rd, Wrexham LL12 7AA
Tel/Ffôn   **+44 (0) 1978 311794**
Web/Y Wê   **www.yale-wrexham.ac.uk**
Drama BTEC Diploma **F**
Dance BTEC Diploma **F**
Technical Theatre BTEC Diploma **F**
Popular & Technical Music BTEC Diploma **F**
Performing Arts National Diploma **F**

Ystrad Mynach College
Twyn Rd, Ystrad Mynach, Mid Glam CF82 7XR
Tel/Ffôn   **+44 (0) 1443 816888**
Web/Y Wê   **www.ystrad-mynach.ac.uk**
Performing Arts National Diploma **F**

OTHER SOURCES OF TRAINING
ERAILL SY'N DARPARU HYFFORDDIANT

Antur Liwt
Groes Efa Bach, Llandyrnog, Dinbych, Sir
Dinbych LL16 4LT
Tel/Ffôn   **+44 (0) 1824 790417**
Email/Ebost   **elis@annwen.freeserve.co.uk**
A company based in Denbigh offering tuition through
the medium of Welsh in the performing arts to
youngsters from 7-17 years of age.
*Mae Antur Liwt yn gwmni newydd sydd wedi ei sefydlu yn
Ninbych i gynnig hyfforddiant tryw gyfrwng y Gymraeg i
blant a phobl ifainc o 7-17 oed yn y celfyddydau
perffformio.*

Arts Training Wales
PO Box 5, Barry, Vale of Glamorgan CF62 3YG
Tel/Ffôn   **+44 (0) 1446 754112**
Fax/Ffacs   **+44 (0) 1446 754113**
Email/Ebost   **admin@a-t-w.com**
Web/Y Wê   **www.a-t-w.com**

Ysgol Glanaethwy
Parc Menai, Bangor, Gwynedd LL57 4BN
Tel/Ffôn   **+44 (0) 1248 671036**
Fax/Ffacs   **+44 (0) 1248 355050**
A Performing Arts School teaching pupils from 6-26
years. They also offer GCSE and A level Drama and
an MA in acting.
*Ysgol berffformio ydi ysgol Glanaethwy sy'n cynnig
hyfforddiant mewn sgiliau theatrig i ddisgyblion o 6-26 oed
Maent hefyd yn dysgu TGAU a Lefel Uwch mewn Drama ac
MA mewn Actio.*

**Many of the venues and organisations listed in
the handbook offer professional, vocational
and informal courses in drama, dance and
stagecraft. Please refer to individual entries
for contact details.**

SUPPLIERS & SERVICES
CYFLENWYR A GWASANAETHAU

GRAPHIC DESIGN
DYLUNIO GRAFFIG

Dylunio Cymru/Design Wales
The Welsh Design Advisory Service,
PO Box 383, Cardiff CF5 2WZ
Tel/Ffôn 0845 3031400 (UK only)
Fax/Ffacs 0845 3031342 (UK only)
Email/Ebost enquiries@wdas.org.uk

fba
4 The Science Park, Aberystwyth SY23 3AH
Tel/Ffôn +44 (0) 1970 636400
Fax/Ffacs +44 (0) 1970 636414
Email/Ebost enqs@fbagroup.co.uk
Web/Y Wê www.fbagroup.co.uk

LICENSING
TRWYDDEDU

Hawliau Perfformio Performing Rights Society
29-33 Berners St, London W1P 4AB
Tel/Ffôn +44 (0) 20 7580 5544
Web/Y Wê www.mcps-prs-alliance.co.uk

MARKETING & PUBLICITY
MARCHNATA A CYHOEDDUSRWYDD

Asbri
Cil y Graig, Hen Durnpike, Tregarth,
Bangor LL57 4NN
Tel/Ffôn +44 (0) 1248 605556

Cardiff Arts Marketing / Marchnata Celfyddydau Caerdydd
2 Market Hse, Market Rd, Canton,
Cardiff CF5 1QE
Tel/Ffôn +44 (0) 29 2037 3736
Fax/Ffacs +44 (0) 29 2038 4141
Email/Ebost mail@cardiff/arts/marketing.co.uk
Web/Y Wê www.arts4cardiff.co.uk

Elinor Wyn Reynolds
38 Penlly Rd, Canton, Cardiff CF5 1NW
Tel/Ffôn +44 (0) 29 2038 8862
Email/Ebost elinorwyn@appleonline.net

Marketing the Arts in Swansea & Carmarthenshire / Marchnata Celfyddydau Abertawe a Sir Caerfyrddin
Parc Howard Museum,
Felinfoel Rd, Llanelli SA153LJ
Tel/Ffôn +44 (0) 1554 755557
Fax/Ffacs +44 (0) 1554 755566
Email/Ebost e-mail@masc.demon.co.uk

Valleys Arts Marketing/ Marchnata Celfyddydau'r Cymoedd
Lower Park Lodge, Sarah Vining-Smith,
Glan Rd, Aberdare CF44 8BN
Tel/Ffôn +44 (0) 1685 884247
Fax/Ffacs +44 (0) 1685 884249
Email/Ebost admin@v-a-m.demon.co.uk
Web/Y Wê valleysartsmarketing.co.uk

Wales Tourist Board – Bwrdd Croeso Cymru
Brunel House, 2 Fitzalan Rd, Cardiff CF24 0UY
Tel/Ffôn +44 (0) 29 2049 9909
Fax/Ffacs +44 (0) 29 2048 5031
Email/Ebost info@tourism.wales.gov.uk
Web/Y Wê www.visitwales.com

TRANSLATORS
CYFIEITHWYR

Afiaith
Is-y-Coed, Tre Taliesin, Machynlleth,
Powys SY20 8JG
Tel/Ffôn +44 (0) 1970 832230
Fax/Ffacs +44 (0) 1970 832230

Asbri
Cil y Graig, Hen Durnpike, Tregarth,
Bangor LL57 4NN
Tel/Ffôn +44 (0) 1248 605556

Cymdeithas Cyfieithwyr Cymru
(The Association of Welsh Translators and Interpreters)
Bryn Menai, Ffordd Caergybi, Bangor,
Gwynedd LL57 2JA
Tel/Ffôn +44 (0) 1248 371839
Fax/Ffacs +44 (0) 1248 371850
Email/Ebost swyddfa@cyfieithwyrcymru.org.uk
info@thewelshtranslators.org.uk

Trosol Gwasanaeth Cyfieithu
CAERDYDD
Unit 1, Cwrt y Parc, Parc Tŷ Glas, Llanisien,
Caerdydd CF14 5GH
Tel/Ffôn +44 (0) 29 2075 0760
Fax/Ffacs +44 (0) 29 2068 1928
Email/Ebost mair@trosol.co.uk
Web/Wê www.trosol.co.uk
CAERNARFON
24-26 Stryd Fawr, Caernarfon LL55 1RH
Tel/Ffôn +44 (0) 1286 673090
Fax/Ffacs +44 (0) 1286 673093
Email/Ebost gwen@trosol.co.uk
Web/Wê www.trosol.co.uk
CASTELL NEWYDD EMLYN
Clôs Sant Ioan, Castell Newydd Emlyn,
Sir Gâr SA38 9AF
Tel/Ffôn +44 (0) 1239 710717
Fax/Ffacs +44 (0) 1239 711181
Email/Ebost enid@trosol.co.uk
Web/Wê www.trosol.co.uk

MEDIA
Y CYFRYNGAU

FILM & TELEVISION
FFILM A THELEDU

Air Force One
The Media Centre, Culverhouse Cross,
Cardiff CF5 6XJ
Tel/Ffôn +44 (0) 29 2059 0123
Fax/Ffacs +44 (0) 29 2059 0123

BAFTA Cymru
Chapter Arts Centre, Market Rd, Canton,
Cardiff CF5 1QE
Tel/Ffôn +44 (0) 29 2022 3898
Fax/Ffacs +44 (0) 29 2066 4189
Email/Ebost post@bafta-cymru.org.uk
Web/Y Wê www.bafta-cymru.org.uk

Barcud Derwen
Cibyn, Caernarfon, Gwynedd LL55 2BD
Tel/Ffôn +44 (0) 1286 671671
Fax/Ffacs +44 (0) 1286 671679
74-78 Park Rd, Whitchurch, Cardiff CF14 7BR
Tel/Ffôn +44 (0) 29 2061 1515
Fax/Ffacs +44 (0) 29 2052 1226
Email/Ebost enq@barcudderwen.com
Web/Y Wê www.barcudderwen.com

BBC Cymru Wales
Broadcasting House, Llantrisant Rd, Llandaff,
Cardiff CF5 2YQ
Tel/Ffôn +44 (0) 29 2032 2000
+44 (0) 1970 833972 Aberystwyth
+44 (0) 1248 370880 Bangor
+44 (0) 1792 654986 Swansea
+44 (0) 1978 221100 Wrexham
Fax/Ffacs +44 (0) 29 2055 2973
Email/Ebost feedback.wales@bbc.co.uk
Web/Y Wê www.bbc.co.uk/wales

Cyfle
Gronant, Penrallt Isaf, Caernarfon LL55 1NS
Tel/Ffôn +44 (0) 1286 671000
Fax/Ffacs +44 (0) 1286 678831
Web/Y Wê www.cyfle.co.uk
Crichton House, 11-12 Mount Stuart Sq,
Cardiff CF10 5EE
Tel/Ffôn +44 (0) 29 2046 5533
Fax/Ffacs +44 (0) 29 2046 3344
Web/Y Wê www.cyfle.co.uk

HTV
The Television Centre, Culverhouse Cross,
Cardiff CF5 6XJ
Tel/Ffôn +44 (0) 29 2059 0590
Fax/Ffacs +44 (0) 29 2059 7183
Email/Ebost htv@htv-wales.com
Web/Y Wê www.htvwales.com
HTV Wales News
Tel/Ffôn +44 (0) 1267 236806 Carmarthen
+44 (0) 1686 623381 Newtown
+44 (0) 1352 755671 Mold
+44 (0) 1492 533502 Colwyn Bay

Independent Television Commission (ITC)
Elgin House, 106 St Mary St, Cardiff CF10 1PA
Tel/Ffôn +44 (0) 29 2038 4541
Fax/Ffacs +44 (0) 29 2022 3157
Email/Ebost stella.thomas@itc.org.uk
Web/Y Wê www.itc.org.uk

ITN
Cardiff Bureau, Media Centre, Culverhouse
Cross, Cardiff CF5 6XJ
Tel/Ffôn +44 (0) 29 2059 0441
Fax/Ffacs +44 (0) 29 2059 0118

Media Skills Wales
Crichton House, 11-12 Mount Stuart Sq,
Cardiff CF10 5EE
Tel/Ffôn +44 (0) 29 2046 5533
Fax/Ffacs +44 (0) 29 2046 3344
Email/Ebost info@mediaskillswales.com
Web/Y Wê www.mediaskillswales.com

Pyramid TV ltd
36 Cardiff Rd, Llandaff, Cardiff CF5 2DR
Tel/Ffôn +44 (0) 29 2057 6888
Fax/Ffacs +44 (0) 29 2057 5777
Email/Ebost info@pyramidtv.co.uk
Web/Y Wê www.pyramidtv.co.uk

S4C Sianel Pedwar Cymru
Parc Tŷ Glas, Llanishen, Cardiff CF14 5DU
Tel/Ffôn +44 (0) 29 2074 7444
Fax/Ffacs +44 (0) 29 2075 4444
Email/Ebost s4c@s4c.co.uk
Web/Y Wê www.s4c.co.uk

Sgrîn,
Media Agency for Wales /
Asiantaeth Cyfryngau Cymru
The Bank, 10 Mount Stuart Sq, Cardiff Bay,
Cardiff CF10 5EE
Tel/Ffôn +44 (0) 29 2033 3300
+44 (0) 1286 671295
Fax/Ffacs +44 (0) 29 2033 3320
+44 (0) 1286 671296
Email/Ebost sgrin@sgrin.co.uk
Web/Y Wê www.sgrin.co.uk

INDEPENDENT FILM & TELEVISION
FFILM A THELEDU ANNIBYNNOL

TAC
Welsh Independent Producers
Caernarfon Office, Gronant, Penrallt Isaf,
Caernarfon LL55 1NS
Tel/Ffôn +44 (0) 1286 671123
Fax/Ffacs +44 (0) 1286 678890
Email/Ebost tac@teledwyr.com
Web/Y Wê www.teledwyr.com
Cardiff Office, Crichton House, 11-12 Mount
Stuart Sq, Cardiff CF10 5EE
Tel/Ffôn +44 (0) 29 2046 3322
Fax/Ffacs +44 (0) 29 2046 3344

N Wales / Gogledd Cymru

Antena	+44 (0) 1286 678592
Cwmni Da	+44 (0) 1286 68530C
Dream Team TV	+44 (0) 1766 780944
Ffilmiau Cenad	+44 (0) 1286 830438
Ffilmiau Gaucho	+44 (0) 1766 514938
Ffilmiau'r Bont	+44 (0) 1286 677225
Ffilmiau'r Nant	+44 (0) 1286 675722
Griffilms	+44 (0) 1286 67667E
Gwdihŵ	+44 (0) 1286 675766
Sianco	+44 (0) 1286 673436
Tonfedd Eryri	+44 (0) 1248 671167

Mid Wales / Canolbarth Cymru

Cwmni Iaith Cyf	+44 (0) 1239 711666
Hon	+44 (0) 1970 615222
Pixel Foundation	+44 (0) 1654 761361
Wes Glei	+44 (0) 1570 471328

S Wales / De Cymru

Acme	+44 (0) 1792 869456
Agenda Television	+44 (0) 1554 880880
Al Fresco	+44 (0) 29 2072 6726
Antena	+44 (0) 29 2031 2000
Atsain	+44 (0) 29 2045 2500
Bangaw	+44 (0) 29 2059 0225
Boda Cyf	+44 (0) 29 2033 3676
Boomerang	+44 (0) 29 2025 0700
Bracan	+44 (0) 29 2033 3200
Cambrensis	+44 (0) 29 2025 7075
Cartwn Cymru	+44 (0) 29 2057 5999
Ci Diog	+44 (0) 29 2066 5050
Cinetig	+44 (0) 29 2048 1420
Concordia cyf	+44 (0) 1554 880880
Cwmni 10	+44 (0) 29 2030 1020
Cynhyrchiadau John Gwyn	+44 (0) 29 2037 8022
Dogo Cymru Ltd	+44 (0) 29 2022 1502
Element Productions	+44 (0) 29 2057 6036
Fflic	+44 (0) 29 2040 9000
Fiction Factory	+44 (0) 29 2030 0320
Genesis Media Group Ltd /Cynhyrchiadau Alan Torjussen Cyf	+44 (0) 29 2062 4669
Green Bay Media	+44 (0) 29 2078 6607
HTV	+44 (0) 29 2059 0590
Mintai	+44 (0) 29 2048 9813
MovieJack	+44 (0) 29 2039 0534
Opus	+44 (0) 29 2022 3456
P.O.P.1	+44 (0) 1554 880880
Penderyn Films Ltd	+44 (0) 29 2049 0781
Siriol Productions	+44 (0) 29 2048 8400
Solo TV	+44 (0) 29 2059 0568
Teledu Apollo	+44 (0) 29 2025 1811
Teledu Avanti	+44 (0) 1443 688227
Teledu Cardinal	+44 (0) 29 2022 8807
Teledu Elidir	+44 (0) 29 2061 0555
Teledu Telesgôp	+44 (0) 1558 823828
Teliesyn	+44 (0) 29 2030 0876
Torpedo Cyf	+44 (0) 29 2076 6117
TracRecord	+44 (0) 29 2021 2130
Tricorn Associates	+44 (0) 1600 860390
Visionthing	+44 (0) 29 2055 1188

RADIO
RADIO

BBC Radio Cymru
Y Ganolfan Ddarlledu, Llandaf,
Cardiff CF5 2YQ
Tel/Ffôn   +44 (0) 29 2032 2018
          +44 (0) 29 2032 2257

BBC Radio Wales
Broadcasting House, Llantrisant Rd Llandaff,
Cardiff CF5 2YQ
Tel/Ffôn   +44 (0) 29 2032 2000
Fax/Ffacs +44 (0) 29 2055 2973
Email/Ebost radio.wales@bbc.co.uk

Bridge FM
PO Box 1063, Bridgend CF31 1WF
Tel/Ffôn   +44 (0) 1656 647777
Fax/Ffacs +44 (0) 1656 673611
Email/Ebost newsroom@bridge.fm
Web/Y Wê   www.bridge.fm

Champion 103 FM
Llys y Dderwen, Parc Menai, Bangor LL57 4BN
Tel/Ffôn   +44 (0) 1248 671888
Fax/Ffacs +44 (0) 1248 671971
Email/Ebost info@championfm.co.uk
Web/Y Wê   www.championfm.co.uk

Coast FM
Media House, 41 Conwy Rd, Colwyn Bay,
Conwy LL28 5AB
Tel/Ffôn   +44 (0) 1492 533733
Fax/Ffacs +44 (0) 1492 535248
Email/Ebost info.coastfm.co.uk
Web/Y Wê   www.coastfm.co.uk

Galaxy 101
Millennium House, 26 Baldwin St,
Bristol BS1 1SE
Tel/Ffôn   +44 (0) 11 7901 0101
Fax/Ffacs +44 (0) 11 7901 4666
Email/Ebost initialsurname@Galaxy101.co.uk
Web/Y Wê   www.Galaxy101.co.uk

Marcher Radio Group Ltd
The Studios, Mold Rd, Gwersyllt,
Wrexham LL11 4AF
Tel/Ffôn   +44 (0) 1978 752202
Fax/Ffacs +44 (0) 1978 759701
Email/Ebost info@mfmradio.co.uk
Web/Y Wê   www.mfmradio.co.uk

Radio Ceredigion
Yr Hen Ysgol Gymraeg, Ffordd Alexandra,
Aberystwyth SY23 1LF
Tel/Ffôn   +44 (0) 1970 627999 Office
Fax/Ffacs +44 (0) 1970 627206
Email/Ebost admin@radioceredigion.f9.co.uk

Radio Maldwyn
The Park, Newtown, Powys SY16 2NZ
Tel/Ffôn   +44 (0) 1686 623555
Fax/Ffacs +44 (0) 1686 623666
Email/Ebost radio.maldwyn@ukonline.co.uk
Web/Y Wê   www.magic756.net

Real Radio
Tŷ Nant Court, Morganstown, Cardiff CF15 8YW
Tel/Ffôn   +44 (0) 29 2031 5100
Fax/Ffacs +44 (0) 29 2031 5151
Email/Ebost info@realradiofm.com
Web/Y Wê   www.realradiofm.com

Red Dragon FM
Atlantic Wharf, Cardiff CF10 4DJ
Tel/Ffôn   +44 (0) 29 2066 2066
Fax/Ffacs +44 (0) 29 2066 2060
Email/Ebost mail@reddragonfm.co.uk
Web/Y Wê   www.reddragonfm.co.uk

Swansea Sound
Victoria Rd, Gowerton, Swansea SA4 3AB
Tel/Ffôn   +44 (0) 1792 511170
Fax/Ffacs +44 (0) 1792 511171
Email/Ebost info@swanseasound.co.uk
Web/Y Wê   www.swanseasound.co.uk

The Wave
PO Box 964, Swansea SA4 3AB
Tel/Ffôn   +44 (0) 1792 511964
Fax/Ffacs +44 (0) 1792 511965
Email/Ebost info@thewave.co.uk
Web/Y Wê   www.thewave.co.uk

Valleys Radio
PO Box 1116, Ebbw Vale NP23 8XW
Tel/Ffôn   +44 (0) 1495 301116
Fax/Ffacs +44 (0) 1495 300710
Email/Ebost admin@valleysradio.co.uk
Web/Y Wê   www.valleysradio.co.uk

Barn
Uned 2, Business Workshops, Cross Hands Business Park, Cross Hands, Llanelli SA14 6RB
Tel/Ffôn   +44 (0) 1269 851640

Big Issue Cymru
55 Charles St, Cardiff CF10 2GD
Tel/Ffôn   +44 (0) 29 2025 5670
Fax/Ffacs   +44 (0) 29 2025 5673
Email/Ebost bigissue@bigissuecymru.fsnet.co.uk

Cambria
PO Box 604, Cardiff CF11 6YD
Tel/Ffôn   +44 (0) 29 2066 7200
Fax/Ffacs   +44 (0) 1267 290188
Email/Ebost cymrica@mcmail.com

Y Cymro
Parc Busnes, Ffordd Wrecsam,
Yr Wyddgrug CH7 1XY
Tel/Ffôn   +44 (0) 1352 707707
Fax/Ffacs   +44 (0) 1352 752180
Email/Ebost nwnfd@netwales.co.uk
Web/Y Wê   www.nwn.co.uk

Daily Post
Vale Rd, Llandudno Junction, Conwy LL31 9SL
Tel/Ffôn   +44 (0) 1492 574455
            +44 (0) 29 2089 8118
Fax/Ffacs   +44 (0) 1492 574433
Email/Ebost news@dailypost.co.uk

Y Faner Newydd
Tŷ'r Ardd, Ffostrasol, Llandysul,
Ceredigion SA44 4SY
Tel/Ffôn   +44 (0) 1239 851555
Email/Ebost fanernewydd@btinternet.com

Golwg
PO Box 4, Lampeter, Ceredigion SA48 7LX
Tel/Ffôn   +44 (0) 1570 423529
Fax/Ffacs   +44 (0) 1570 423538
Email/Ebost ymholiadau@golwg.com
Web/Y Wê   www.golwg.com

New Welsh Review
Chapter Arts Centre, Market Rd, Canton, Cardiff CF5 1QE
Tel/Ffôn   +44 (0) 29 2066 5529
Fax/Ffacs   +44 (0) 29 2066 5529
Email/Ebost nwr@welshnet.co.uk
Web/Y Wê   www.academi.org

Onewales
Thomson House, Havelock St, Cardiff CF10 1XR
Tel/Ffôn   +44 (0) 29 2058 3475
Fax/Ffacs   +44 (0) 29 2058 3518
Email/Ebost onewales@wme.co.uk
Web/Y Wê   www.icwales.co.uk

Planet
The Welsh Internationalist
PO Box 44, Aberystwyth, Ceredigion SY23 3ZZ
Tel/Ffôn   +44 (0) 1970 611255
Fax/Ffacs   +44 (0) 1970 611197
Email/Ebost planet.enquries@planetmagazine.org.uk
Web/Y Wê   www.planetmagazine.org.uk

Poetry Wales
38-40 Nolton St, Bridgend CF31 3BN
Tel/Ffôn   +44 (0) 1656 663018
Fax/Ffacs   +44 (0) 1656 649226
Email/Ebost poetrywales@seren.force9.co.uk
Web/Y Wê   www.seren-books.com

Taliesin
c/o Academi, 3rd Flr, Mount Stuart House, Mount Stuart Square, Cardiff CF10 5FQ
Tel/Ffôn   +44 (0) 29 2047 2266
Fax/Ffacs   +44 (0) 29 2049 2930
Email/Ebost post@academi.org
Web/Y Wê   www.academi.org

Welsh Living
Media House, 5 Llys Fedwen, Parc Menai, Bangor LL57 4BF
Tel/Ffôn   +44 (0) 1248 679003
Fax/Ffacs   +44 (0) 1248 679106
Email/Ebost info@welshliving.com

The Western Mail
Thomson House, Havelock St, Cardiff CF10 1XR
Tel/Ffôn   +44 (0) 29 2022 3333
Fax/Ffacs   +44 (0) 29 2058 3652
Email/Ebost newsdesk@wme.co.uk
Web/Y Wê   www.icwales.co.uk

WM Magazine
Thomson House, Havelock St, Cardiff CF10 1XR
Tel/Ffôn   +44 (0) 29 2058 3475
Fax/Ffacs   +44 (0) 29 2058 3518
Email/Ebost cewilliams@wme.co.uk
Web/Y Wê   www.icwales.co.uk

DAILY NEWSPAPERS
PAPURAU NEWYDD DYDDIOL

Shropshire Star
Ketley, Telford TF1 5HU
Tel/Ffôn   +44 (0) 1952 242424
Fax/Ffacs   +44 (0) 1952 254605
Email/Ebost newsroom@shropstar.co.uk
Web/Y Wê   www.shropshirestar.com

South Wales Argus
Cardiff Rd, Maesglas, Newport NP20 3QN
Tel/Ffôn   +44 (0) 1633 810000
Fax/Ffacs   +44 (0) 1633 777202
Email/Ebost newsdesk@gwent.wales.co.uk
Web/Y Wê   www.thisisgwent.co.uk

South Wales Echo
Thomson House, Havelock St, Cardiff CF10 1XR
Tel/Ffôn   +44 (0) 29 2022 3333
Fax/Ffacs   +44 (0) 29 2058 3624
Email/Ebost letters@wme.co.uk
Web/Y Wê   www.icwales.co.uk

South Wales Evening Post
PO Box 14, Adelaide St, Swansea SA1 1QT
Tel/Ffôn   +44 (0) 1792 510000
Fax/Ffacs   +44 (0) 1792 514697
Email/Ebost postbox@swwp.co.uk
Web/Y Wê   www.thisissouthwales.co.uk

Western Daily Press
Temple Way, Old Market, Bristol BS99 7HD
Tel/Ffôn   +44 (0) 11 7934 3000
Fax/Ffacs   +44 (0) 11 7934 3574
Email/Ebost wdculture@bepp.co.uk
Web/Y Wê   www.westpress.co.uk

Wrexham Evening Leader
Centenary Bldgs, King St, Wrexham LL11 1PN
Tel/Ffôn   +44 (0) 1978 355151
Fax/Ffacs   +44 (0) 1978 311421
Email/Ebost nwnfd@netwales.co.uk
Web/Y Wê   www.nwn.co.uk

LOCAL NEWSPAPERS
PAPURAU NEWYDD LLEOL

N Wales / Gogledd Cymru

Abergele & St Asaph Visitor, Rhyl & Prestatyn Visitor	+44 (0) 1492 584321
Bangor & Anglesey Mail	+44 (0) 1286 671111
Caernarfon & Denbigh Herald	+44 (0) 1286 671111
Chester & District Standard	+44 (0) 1244 351234
Chronicle Series (Flintshire)	+44 (0) 1244 821911
Corwen Times	+44 (0) 1678 520262
Y Cyfnod (Y Seren / N Wales Star)	+44 (0) 1678 520262
Denbighshire Free Press	+44 (0) 1745 813535
Y Dydd	+44 (0) 1341 422547
Flintshire Leader & Standard	+44 (0) 1352 707707
Yr Herald / Papurau'r Herald Series	+44 (0) 1286 671111
Llandudno Advertiser	+44 (0) 1492 584321
Merioneth Express	+44 (0) 1678 520262
Mold & Buckley Chronicle	+44 (0) 1352 755455
Mold & Deeside Midweek Leader	+44 (0) 1352 707707
N Wales Chronicle Series	+44 (0) 1248 387400
N Wales Pioneer	+44 (0) 1492 531188
N Wales Weekly News	+44 (0) 1492 584321
Rhyl Prestatyn & Abergele Journal	+44 (0) 1745 357500
This Week Wales	+44 (0) 1766 540250
The Vale Advertiser	+44 (0) 1745 815454
Wrexham Leader	+44 (0) 1978 355151
Wrexham Mail	+44 (0) 1978 351515

Mid Wales / Canolbarth Cymru

Brecon & Radnor Express & Powys County Times	+44 (0) 1874 623230
Cambrian News	+44 (0) 1970 615000
Cardigan & Tivyside Advertiser	+44 (0) 1239 614343
Carmarthen Journal	+44 (0) 1267 227222
County Echo Newspapers Ltd	+44 (0) 1348 874445
County Times Express & Gazette Series	+44 (0) 1938 553354
Llanelli Star Series	+44 (0) 1554 745300
Mid Wales Journal	+44 (0) 1743 248248
Milford Mercury Series	+44 (0) 1646 698971
The North Ceredigion Times	+44 (0) 1970 615000
Shrewsbury Chronicle	+44 (0) 1743 248248
S Wales Guardian	+44 (0) 1269 592781
Tenby Observer / Narberth & Whitland Observer	+44 (0) 1834 843262
Western Telegraph	+44 (0) 1437 763133

S Wales / De Cymru

Abergavenny Chronicle	+44 (0) 1873 852187
Barry & District News	+44 (0) 1446 733456
Bridgend & Valleys Recorder / Porthcawl & District Recorder	+44 (0) 1656 669330
Caerphilly Campaign Series	+44 (0) 29 2085 1100
Cardiff Post Series	+44 (0) 29 2058 3470
Cynon Valley Leader	+44 (0) 1685 873136
The Free Press Series	+44 (0) 1495 751133
Free Press Series (Wales)	+44 (0) 1633 810000
Glamorgan Gazette Series	+44 (0) 1656 304900
Glamorgan Gem Ltd	+44 (0) 1446 774484
Gwent Gazette	+44 (0) 1495 304589
Merthyr Express Series	+44 (0) 1685 856506
Monmouthshire Beacon	+44 (0) 1600 712142
Neath Guardian & Port Talbot Guardian	+44 (0) 1639 778887
Penarth Times	+44 (0) 29 2070 7234
Pioneer Press (Wales) Ltd	+44 (0) 1639 895901
Pontypridd & Llantrisant Observer	+44 (0) 1443 665161
Port Talbot Tribune Series	+44 (0) 1639 891223
Rhondda Leader	+44 (0) 1443 665151
The Ross Gazette	+44 (0) 1989 562007
Swansea Herald of Wales	+44 (0) 1792 514999

red snapper
theatre photography & web design

keith morris

34 stryd cambria | aberystwyth | ceredigion | sy23 1nz

phone: +44 (0)1970 611106
fax: +44 (0)1970 611234
mobile: (07710) 285 968

keith@artx.co.uk

www.red-snapper-web.co.uk   www.red-snapper.co.uk   www.theatre-wales.co.uk

Appendices

ATODIADAU

NEW PLAYS 1991 - 2002 DRAMÂU NEWYDD

Actors Touring Company

year	title	author	cast size
1991	Woman of Flowers	Sion Eiran	5

Alma Theatre Company details on page 10

year	title	author	cast size
1994	The Belly	devised by the company	4
1995	The Dress	devised by the company	4
1998	You Are Now Here	devised by the company	4

Cwmni Theatr Arad Goch Company details on page 11

year	title	author	cast size
1991	Dyn Mawr, Dyn Bach, y Dewin a'r Doctor	Angharad Tomos	4
	Growing/Tyfu	Jeremy Turner/Catherine Aran	2
	Hel Meddyliau/Winter Pictures	devised by the company	2
1992	Dygymod	Mari Rhian Owen	2
	Cip Coeden a Chant	Gwen Lasarus	4
1993	Ty Ni	Gareth Ioan	4
	Yn ein Dwylo	Pam Palmer	9
	Ffrwgwd y Tad a'r mab ... neu ... Rhydd i Bawb ei Bimpyls	John Glyn Owen	4
1994	Hyn Oll yn ei Chalon	Mari Rhian Owen	1
	Lleuad yn Olau/One Moonlit Night	devised by the company	4
	Rhyfel y Sais Bach	devised by the company/Gill Ogden	3
	Cerdyn Post o Wlad Rwla	Angharad Tomos	4
1995	Drosy Garreg/Over the Stone	Mari Rhian Owen	2
	Sgrech	Gareth Ioan	4
	Aderyn glas mewn bocs sgidiau	Siân Summers	1
	Nid Fi/Not Me	Mari Rhian Owen	3
	Taliesin	devised by the company/Jeremy Turner	5
1996	Rushes	Lucy Gough	3
1997	Dyrchafiad Dyn Bach... neu ... Anna Mari Lyfs Dic Wili	John Glyn Owen	4
	Merched y Gerddi/Garden Girls	Mari Rhian Owen	3
	Morys y Gwynt ac Ifan y Glaw	Jeremy Turner	3
	Yn y Dechreuad/In The Beginning	devised by the company/Jeremy Turner	3
1998	Cwrw Chips a Darlith Deg	Siân Summers	1
	Parachutes and Petticoats	devised by the company/Sêra Moore Williams	3
	Rownd y Byd Mewn Lori	Sêra Moore Williams	2
	3D	devised by Theatr Iolo	4
	Clychau'r Môr/Sailors' Bells and the Big Big Waves	devised by the company/Jeremy Turner	5
	The Good Brig Credo	Mari Rhian Owen	3
	Sioe Rwtsh Rala Rwdins	Angharad Tomos	4

1999	Hen Het/Old Hat	Jeremy Turner/Mari Rhian Owen	1
	Ma's o 'Ma	devised by the company/Sêra Moore Williams	3
	Dilema	gan Lab I	3
2000	Culhwch ac Olwen/The Giant's Daughter	devised by the company/Jeremy Turner	5

Bara Caws Company details on page 13

year	title	author	cast size
1991	Y Gweledigaethau	devised by the company	6
	Fi a Mr Louigi	Mair Griffith	4
1992	Tweileit Zon	Twm Miall	4
	Lawr y Lon	Myrddin Ap Dafydd	4
	Chwarae'r Diawl	Mair Gruffydd	4
1993	Chwilen yn fy Mhen	Mair Gruffydd	3
	Siarad ar eu Cyfer	Twm Miall	5
1994	Rhosyn a Rhych	Twm Miall	5
	Diana	John Glyn Owen	5
1995	Cyw Dol	Twm Miall	5
	Yn Debyg Iawn i ti a fi	Meic Povey	4
	Un Bach Arall	Twm Miall	4
	Darn-Gae	Twm Miall	4
	Y Wraig & Bobi a Sami	W S Jones	4
1996	Lliferiau	W S Jones	4
	Henwaliau	Mari Gwilym	3
1997	Brodyr a Brwsh/Brothers of the Brush	trans Tony Llewelyn/Jimmy Murphy	4
	Y Swedjan a'r Smacyrs	Bryn Fon/Twm Miall	4
	Dinas Barhaus	W S Jones	4
1998	Oedolion yn Unig	Robin Gruffydd/Dyfed Thomas	1
	Paris	John Godber trans Bryn Fon	3
	Bargen	devised by the company	5
	Y Folsan Fawr	Robin Griffith/Dyfed Thomas	5
1999	Hardcore Bethesda Fuzz	Dyfrig Jones	4
	Sundance	Aled Jones Willliams	1
	Yr Almo	Bryn Fon	5
2000	Paradwys Waed	Sion Eirian	5
	Dj Ffawst	adpt Elinor Wyn Reynolds	5
	Al a Dorothy	Twm Miall	4
2001	Ben Set	W S Jones	3
	Bingo Bach	Sian Summers	4
	Lliwau Rhyddid	Ifor ap Glyn/Elinor Wyn Reynolds	2
2002	Mwnci Nel	Derec Thomas	5

Brith Gof

year	title	author	cast size
1991	Gwynt, Glaw, Glo a Defaid		-
	(Wind, Rain, Coal and Sheep)		
	Displaced persons	devised by the company	-
	Los Angeles II	devised by the company	4
	From Memory	devised by the company	-
	Pax	devised by the company	5
1992	Patagonia	devised by the company	5
	In Black and White	devised by the company	-
	Los Angeles III	devised by the company	-
	Ar y Traeth (On the Beach)	devised by the company	5
	Der Gefesselte (The Bound Man)	devised by the company	-
	Haearn	devised by the company	-
1993	DOA	devised by the company	-
	Camlann	devised by the company	6
	I lythyron o'r Nefoedd	devised by the company	6
1994	Angelus	devised by the company	-
	Cusanu Esgyrn	devised by the company	-
	Arturius Rex	devised by the company	-
1995	Y Pen Bas Y Pen Dwfn	devised by the company	4
	Tri Bywyd	devised by the company	5
1996	Prydain	devised by the company	7
	Once Upon a Time in the West	devised by the company	3
	Sawl Bywyd	devised by the company	-
1997	Hafod	devised by the company	5
	Dead Men's Shoes	devised by the company	1
1998	Llais Cynan	devised by the company	-
1999	Dyddiau Olaf Dyddiau Cyntaf	devised by the company	5
	I am Here on False Pretences	devised by the company	-
2000	Draw Draw yn ...	devised by the company	-

Theatre y Byd Company details on page 14

year	title	author	cast size
1994	Thinking In Welsh	Dafydd Wyn Roberts	1
	The Change	Jane Buckler/Helen Griffin	1
	Big Black Hole	Tim Rhys	1
	Gobeithion Gorffwyl	Sharon Morgan	1
	Glissando on an Empty Harp	Ian Rowlands	4
	Love in Plastic	Ian Rowlands	4
1996	Marriage of Convenience	Ian Rowlands	1
1999	Blue Heron in the Womb	Ian Rowlands	5
	New South Wales	Ian Rowlands	2
2001	Mor Tawel / Pacific	Ian Rowlands	1

Castaway Community Theatre Company

year	title	author	cast size
1996	Lola Brecht	Dic Edwards	large cast
2001	Mapping the Soul	Lucy Gough	large cast

Clwyd Theatr Cymru Company details on page 16

year	title	author	cast size
1992	Facing Up	Ieuan Watkin	-
1993	Full Moon	Caradoc Pritchard adapt	6
		John Owen/Helen Kaut Howson	
1994	As To Be Naked	Lucy Gough	4
	August	Anton Chekhov, adpt Julian Mitchell	11
1996	Double Indemnity	James M Cain, adpt David Joss Buckley	7
	Silas Marner	George Elliot, adpt Greg Cullen	7
1997	Cinderella: The Panto With Soul	Peter Rowe/Alan Ellis	10
1997	Rape of the Fair Country	Alexander Cordell, adapt Manon Eames	16
1998	The Journey of Mary Kelly	Sian Evans	14
	The Changeling	Greg Cullen	3
	Celf	Yasmina Reza, trans Manon Eames	3
1999	Aladdin-The Wok 'n' Roll Panto	Peter Rowe/Alan Ellis	10
	Hosts of Rebecca	Alexander Cordell, adapt Manon Eames	14
	Song of the Earth	Alexander Cordell, adapt Manon Eames	16
	Flora's War/Rhyfel Flora	Tim Baker	4
	An Evening with Charles Dickens	Charles Dickens, adpt Richard Moore	1
2000	Dick Whittington &	Peter Rowe/Alan Ellis	10
	the Coolest Cat in Town		
	Word for Word/Gair am Air	Tim Baker	4
	Hard Times	Charles Dickens, adpt Manon Eames	9
	Damwain a Hap	Dario Fo, adpt Manon Eames	9
2001	The Secret/Y Gyfrinach	Tim Baker	4
	The Rabbit	Meredydd Barker	6
	Jack and the Beanstalk	Peter Rowe/Alan Ellis	10

Y Cwmni

year	title	author	cast size
1989	House of America	Ed Thomas	5
	Adar heb Adennydd	Ed Thomas	7
1990	The Myth of Michael Roderick	Ed Thomas	7
	East from the Gantry	Ed Thomas	3
1991	Flowers of the Dead Red Sea	Ed Thomas	3
1998	Gas Station Angel	Ed Thomas	9

Dalier Sylw

year	title	author	cast size
1991	Mysgu Cymyle	Branwen Cennard	6
1992	Simone Weil, Y Forwyn Goch	Menna Elfyn	6
1994	Calon Ci	Gareth Miles	7
	Epa yn y Parlwr Cefn	Sion Eirian	4
1995	Y Cinio	Geraint Lewis	5
	Fel Anifail	Meic Povey	2
	The Language of Heaven	Geraint Lewis	5
1996	Y Grosffordd	Geraint Lewis	4
	Meindiwch Eich Busnes	Geraint Lewis	1
1997	Bonansa	Meic Povey	5
	Spam Man	Dafydd Llewelyn	3
	Cnawd	Aled Jones Williams	2
	Maoysata	Sêra Moore Williams	8
1998	Tair	Meic Povey	3
1999	Y Madogwys	Gareth Miles	10
2000	Radio Cymru	Wiliam Owen Roberts	5

Eddie Ladd (Jesus & Tracy) Company details on page 20

year	title	choreographer	cast size
1993	Callas sings mad songs	Eddie Ladd (Jesus & Tracy)	4
1994	Unglucklicherweise	Eddie Ladd & Roger Owen	2
1996	Once upon a time in the west	Eddie Ladd with Brith Gof	3
1998	Lla'th	Eddie Ladd in collaboration with Clifford McLucas	1 + 10
2000	Scarface	Eddie Ladd / Aphina Vahla	1

Elan Wales Company details on page 21

year	title	author	cast size
1991	The Last Ferry	devised	120
	The Mud Vision	devised	25
1992	Der Aufbruch zum Untergang	F Guidi	20
	Eating the Gods	devised	25
	Raw Women & Cooked Men 1	F Guidi	3
	Masking of the City	devised	150
1993	Raw Women & Cooked Men 2	F Guidi	6
	Time in a Red Coat	impulse G. Mackay Brown	16
	The Song of Iron on Stone	impulse G.Mackay Brown	20
	The Garden of Delights	devised	4
1994	Eine Schlaflose Nacht	F Guidi	6
	Evil Bakes a Cherry Pie	F Guidi	3
	Dying to Curse	devised	15
	Bouquet of Back-handed Compliments	F Guidi	16
	Madame Joy	F Guidi	20
1995	Bombs and Bloomers	F Guidi	15
	Dyhead	devised	18
	Cariad	F Guidi	20
	And the Dragon was a Queen at Last	F Guidi	3
	Raw Women and Cooked Men 3	F Guidi	6
	Eine Kurze Gecshichte der Menschheit	devised	6
	The Bone Shoes	F Guidi	16
	Lacrime e Boogie	F Guidi	2
	Leere Saite	F Guidi	6
1996	Raw Women and Cooked Men 3	F Guidi	6
	Evil Bakes a Cherry Pie	F Guidi	3
	Icona Zero	devised	16
	Sarajevo Steel	F Guidi	4
	O et Nous	devised	10
1996	The Tree Brides	F Guidi	15
	The Tidefields	F Guidi	25
	Glamstock	devised	20
1997	Greasepaint & Lemon Polonecks	F. Guidi	25
	Die Heilige Kummernis	devised	7
	Scharlachgold	F Guidi	6
	Of Love and Demons	F Guidi	18
	Acqua Nera	F Guidi	30
1998	Shadows in the Ditch	F Guidi	45
	Land of Heart's Desire	F Guidi	19
	Sharlachgold	F Guidi	6
	Mamo Miri	devised	17
	Sangue del Mio Sangue	F Guidi	26
	In the Name of the Body	F Guidi	15

All the Sundays of May	F Guidi	6
Fear no Man's Return	F Guidi	20
1999 The Hidden God	devised	30
Divine Wills	devised	26
The Cloud of Unknowing	F Guidi	10
Skin Traffic	F Guidi	16
Duende	F Guidi	16
Cybermama	F Guidi	17
2000 In My Mouth	F Guidi	12
State of Grace	F Guidi	35
Transit Sheds	devised	26
Metamorfosi	from Ovid by F Guidi	24
Faust	Goethe by F Guidi	36
R.ex	F Guidi	20
The Cut	F Guidi	4
2001 Prince of Fire	Shakespeare, adpt	35
Steamed Pork Pies	F. Guidi	18
Vinyl	Shakespeare adpt F Guidi	12
RAM	devised	14
H20	Shakespeare adpt F Guidi	36
Hamlet In Loving Memory	F Guidi	35

Equilibre Company details on page 22

year	title	author	cast size
1993	Equilibre	devised by the company	16
1994	Du'r Moroedd	devised by the company	14
1995	Awakening	Nigel Wells/The company	8
1996	Equilibre '96	devised by the company	5
1997	Shaping Shadows	devised by the company	5
1998	Revolution	devised by the company	7
1999	Khazars	devised by the company	7
2001	Horse	devised from poem by Ronald Duncan	5

Equinox Theatre

year	title	author	cast size
1998	Dorothy Squires	Mark Ryan	-
1999	Castradiva	Mark Ryan	1

Fallen Angel

year	title	author	cast size
1994	Crossing the Bar	Lucy Gough/Ashley Wallington	3
	Fallen Angel	Ashley Wallington	2

Fiction Factory

year	title	author	cast size
1993	Envy	Ed Thomas	1
1994	Hiraeth/Strangers in Conversation	Ed Thomas	2
1995	Song From a Forgotten City	Ed Thomas	3

Cwmni'r Frân Wen Company details on page 23

year	title	author	cast size
1991	Diffinia	Angharad Tomos	4
	Trwy Gicio a Brathu	devised by the company	4
1992	Caru O.K.	Mair Gruffydd	4
	Amyswn	devised by the company	4
1993	Yn dy Law	devised by the company	3
	Newid Bach	devised by the company	4
	Copacoco	devised by the company	3
1994	Melangell	devised by the company	4
	Mud Losgi	Lousie Osbourn adpt Iola Ynyr	4
	Yr Arth a'r Blaidd	Eirwen Hopkins	3
1995	Yma o Hud	devised by the compnay	3
	Codi Gwrychyn	devised by the company	3
	Yr Aur Gwyn	devised by the company	3
1996	Torri Geiriau	devised by the company	3
	Ffeirio	Iola Ynyr	3
	Chwarae Byw	Iola Ynyr	3
1997	Anne Frank	Iola Ynyr	4
	Gwneud Môr a Mynydd	Sian Summers	3
	Faciwi	Sian Summers	3
1998	John Evans	Ffion Emlyn	3
	Cyffordd	Iola Ynyr	4
1999	Lyfli	Iola Ynyr	4
	Trefn a Dysgeidiaeth	Iola Ynyr	2
	Ti a Fi	Iola Ynyr	2
2000	Cae o Adar Duon/	Kevin Dyer	3
	The Field of Blackbirds	trans Meinir Lynch	
	Snog Spar	Dafydd Llewelyn	3
	Lleisiau yn y Parc	Iola Ynyr	2
2001	Chwarae Plant	Iola Ynyr	3

Frantic Assembly

year	title	author	cast size
1995	Klub	Spencer Hazel	6
1996	Flesh	Spencer Hazel	4
1997	Zero	Devised by the company	5
1998	Sell Out	Michael Wynne	4

Goodcop Badcop Company details on page 24

year	title	author	cast size
	The White Room	devised by the company	4
1996	Closing Down Sale	devised by the company	3
1998	Loop	devised by the company	5
2000	Homeopathic Pornography	devised by the company	1

Green Ginger Company details on page 25

year	title	author	cast size
1990	Gaston - Street performance	Chris Pirie/Terry Lee	2
	Frank Einstein-Born to be Wired	Chris Pirie/Terry Lee	2
1997	Slaphead - Demon Barber	devised by the company	4
1999	Bambi - The Wilderness Years	devised by the company	4

Gwent Theatre Company details on page 26

year	title	author	cast size
1991	After Hours	devised by the company	6
	The Watching	devised by the company	5
1992	The Watchport Quilt	devised by the company	4
	Gwreiddiau	Sêra Moore Williams	4
	Deadline	Andy Andrews	5
1993	Body of Principles	devised by the company	6
	Y Dilyw	Charles Way	4
	Y Gorlan	Sêra Moore Williams	4
1994	Dead Mans Hat	Charles Way	5
	Uncertain Lives	John Lovat	5
1995	Teithiau	Theatr Iolo	32
	Still Waters	devised by the company	5
	Y Garreg Ddu	Theatr West Glamorgan	3
1996	Time and Time Again	Mike James	5
	Home Front	Philip Michel	3
	Marchogion yn y Dinas	Theatr Iolo	-
1997	Land of Dreams	devised by the company	4
	The Good Old Days	devised by the company	4
	Words,Words,Words	Philip Michell	3
1998	How High is Up	Brendan Murray	4
	Sibrwd yn y Nos	Noel Greig	4
	Whispers in the Dark	Noel Greig	-
1999	A Spell of Cold Weather	Charles Way	4
	Skylark Song	Philip Michell	3
	The Reincarnations of	Elizabeth & Philip Michell	3
2000	Pa Mor Uchel yw Fyny	Brendan Murray	4
	Miriad, A Boy From Bosnia	Ad de Bont	2
	Sonya and the Dancing Bear	Mark Ryan	3
	In Living Memory	Charles Wray	50
2001	Y Ddraig Hud	Mike Kenny	2
	Voice	Tracey Spottiswoode	3
	Common Threads	Alex Pascall	5

Cwmni Theatr Gwynedd Company details on page 27

year	title	author	cast size
1991	Dim Ond Heno	Gwion Lynch	6
1993	Golff	William R Lewis	7
	Chwith Meddwl	Richard T Jones	3
	Awe Bryncoch	Mei Jones	8
1995	Cwm Glo Kitchener	adapt Manon Rhys	7
1996	Jeli Bebis	Miriam Llywelyn	6
	Tua'r Terfyn	Iwan Edgar	7
1997	Yr Aduniad	Delyth Jones	6
	Y Bandit, y Barwn,	Arwel Roberts/Emlyn Roberts	8
	a'r Boi Bananas		
	Sion Blewyn Coch	John Ogwen	7
1998	Pel Goch	Aled Jones Williams	2
	Bownsars	trans Meirion Davies	5
	Tri Chryfion Byd	Emlyn Roberts	4
1999	Oleanna - Mamet	adapt Gareth Miles	2
	Ffrwd Ceinwen	William R Lewis	6
	Wal	Aled Jones Williams	2
	Plant Gladys	Sêra Moore Williams	2
	Diwedd y Byd	Meic Povey	4
	Yr Hen Blant	Meic Povey	5
2000	Comin Jac	Emlyn Roberts	5
2001	Wal a Tiwlips	Aled Jones Williams	2-3

Y Gymraes Company details on page 28

year	title	author	cast size
1992	Byth Rhy Hwyr	Sêra Moore Williams	3
1994	Trais Tyner	Sêra Moore Williams	5
1995	Mae Sian yn Gadael Cymru	Sêra Moore Williams	5
1998	Mefus	Sêra Moore Williams	2
2000	Mor Forwyn	Sêra Moore Williams	4
2001	Mab	Sêra Moore Williams	3

Hijinx Theatre Company details on page 29

year	title	author	cast size
1991	Taking Flight	devised by the company	3
	The House at the Edge of the World	devised by the company	3
1992	Touch and Go	devised by the company	3
	One for Sorrow	devised by the company	4
1993	Down to Earth	devised by the company	3
	In The Bleak Midwinter	Charles Way	4
1994	On the Road Again	Laurence Allen	2
	Carpet of Dreams	devised by the company/Theatr Iolo	3
	Ill met by Moonlight	Charles Way	4
1995	Bombs and Bloomers	devised by the company/Elan/community	12
	Promises, Promises	devised by the company	3
	Stairway to Heaven	Laurence Allan	-
1996	Give Us a Chance	devised by the company/community	3
	A Leap in The Dark	Brendan Murray	4
	On the Road Again	Laurence Allan	2
	The Dove Maiden	Charles Way	4
1997	Greasepaint and Lemon Polonecks	devised by the company /Elan	24
	Wishful Thinking	devised by the company	3
	Dangerous Acquaintances	Laurence Allan	4
	On the Road Again	Laurence Allan	2
1998	In the Blink of an Eye	devised by the company	12
	A Room of my Own	Philip Michell	3
	All the Sundays of May	Firenza Guidi	4
1999	Springboard	devised by the company/Community	large
	Set Up	devised by the company/Community	large
	Paul Robeson Knew My Father	Greg Cullen	4
2000	Out of Fear	devised by the company	3
	The Other Robinson Crusoe	devised by the company/Community	14
	Tarzanne - Queen of the Valley	Greg Cullen	4
2001	To have and to Hold	devised by the company	4

Theatr Iolo Company details on page 31

year	title	author	cast size
1991	The Storytelling Stone	devised	3
	Gwreiddiau	Sêra Moore Williams	5
1992	Leonardo	devised	3
	Journey	devised	3
	By a Thread	Lucy Gough	4
1993	Garden of Delights	devised	4
	City of Dreams	devised	4
1994	Carpet of Dreams	devised	3
1995	Rough Magic	devised	4
	The Carpet, The Cook & Cockatoo	devised	4
	Watchers of the Night Sky	Lucy Gough	3
	Carreg Haneision	devised	3
1996	Box of Fear	devised	4
	Knights in the City	Philip Michell	3
1997	The Party	devised	4
	Avo Penn	devised	3
	Gwrthryfel	devised	4
	Days with Frog and Toad	adpt	3
	3D	devised	4
1998	Half a Pound of Treacle	Phillip Michell	3
	The Rock	Peter Rumney	4
1999	The Lost Boys	Paul Conway	5
	Telling Tales	devised	3
2000	Marcos	Kevin Lewis	1
	The Stringman	devised	3
	Box of Secrets	-	3
2001	Mole in a Hole	Glenys Evans/Kevin Lewis	2
2001	Bison & Sons	Pauline Mol trans Rina Vergano	

Lurking Truth Company details on page 32

year	title	author	cast size
1996	The Back of Beyond	David Ian Rabey	13
1997	Bite or Suck	David Ian Rabey	2
1998	The Battle of the Crows	David Ian Rabey	10
2001	The Twelfth Battle of Isonzo	Howard Barker	2

Made In Wales

year	title	author	cast size
1995	Nothing to Pay	Simon Harris	10
1996	Safar	Afshan Malik	5
	The Sea that Blazed	Christine Watkins	4
	Little Sister	Sian Evans	5
1997	Cradle to the grave	Larry Allan	12+
	Love in Aberdare	Roger Williams, James Williams	15+
	Calon Lan	Roger Williams	
	Gulp	Roger Williams	5
	Baywatch Cymru	Patrick Prior	5
1998	My Piece of Happiness	Lewis Davies	5
	Cenedl Fach, Rhyfel Mawr	Lewis Davies, Kate O'Reilly Roger Williams and company	15+
	Queen of Hearts	Christine Watkins	4
	Dare	Tracy Spottiswoode, Tim Riley	15+
	Giant Steps	Othniel Smith	3
1999	Lives of Seahorses	Leslie Ash	5
	Killing Kangaroos	Roger Williams	7
	More Life	Based on Stereophonis song	12+
2000	Dad to Damnation	Peter Morgan, Mark Ryan	4

The Magdalena Project

year	title	author	cast size
1996	Child	Jill Greenhalgh	1

Music Theatre Wales Company details on page 34

year	title	author	cast size
1994	Flowers	text Ed Thomas	3
1995	The Soldier's Tale	Sion Eirian	3
1997	The Roswell Incident	libretto Heledd Wyn	4
2000	Jane Eyre	composer Michael Berkeley	5

Theatr Na N'og Company details on page 35

year	title	author	cast size
1991	Working It Out	devised by the company	3
	Smiling through	devised by the company	4
	Adar o'r Unlliw	devised by the company	3
	Baled y Garreg Ddu	devised by the company	3
1992	All Sewn Up	devised by the company	3
	Playing it by 'ere	devised by the compnay	3
1993	Killjoy	Helen Griffin	3
	Para 'mlaen	devised by the company	3
	Dawns y Dodo	devised by the company	2
1994	Combrogos	devised by the company	6
	Clustie Mawr Moch Bach	devised by the company	4
1995	Timelines	devised by the company	3
1996	I'r Byw	devised by the company	5
	20.20	devised by the company	3
	Straeon Groeg/Greek Myths	adpt Geinor Jones	2
1997	Rape of the Fair Country	adpt Manon Eames	8
1998	Pedwar Ban y Byd/Four Corners	Geinor Jones	2
	Codi Stem/Full Steam Ahead	Lynne Jones	3
1999	1 + 1	Jeremy Cockram	2
	Jac Tar	adpt Geinor Jones	3
2000	Brodyr y Garreg Ddu/ Brothers and Black Diamonds	adpt Geinor Jones	3
	Spam Man	Dafydd Llewelyn	3
2001	Ssshhh!	Ioan Hefin	2

Pearson / Brookes Company details on page 37

year	title	author	cast size
1997	Dead Men's Shoes	Mike Pearson/Mike Brookes	1
1998	The First Five Miles	Mike Pearson/Mike Brookes	1
	Body of Evidence	Mike Pearson/Mike Brookes	1
	The man who ate his boots	Mike Pearson/Mike Brookes	1
1999	Just a bit of history repeating	Mike Pearson/Mike Brookes	1
2000	Like a pelican in the wilderness (towards the north: act 1)	Mike Pearson/Mike Brookes	5
2001	Carrying On	Mike Pearson/Mike Brookes	-

Theatr Powys Company details on page 38

year	title	author	cast size
1992	The Emperors New Clothes	devised by the company	4
	Soil	devised by the company	4
	Red Dressing	Louise Osborn	4
	Regan	Dic Edwards	5
	Raging Angels	Greg Cullen	8
	The Last Days of Don Juan	Tirso de Molina	30
	Mother Hubbard	Dic Edwards	6
1993	Sharazade	devised by the company	4
	The Present	devised by the company	4
	Coch du ac Anwybodus	Edward Bond	4
	Clouds of Glory	Mary Cooper	4
	The Last Picnic	devised by the company	3
	Lysistrata Aristophones	Youth Community	20
1994	Gogoniant	Mary Cooper	4
	The Caretakers Plot	devised by the company	3
	Llain y Gofalwr	devised by the company	3
	Little Devils	Greg Cullen	40
	The Partridge Dance	Geoff Gillham	4
	Rumplestiltskin	Mike Kenny	6
1995	The Hunter's Field	devised by the company	3
	I Bravi Ragazzi	Carys Evans	4
	Tua'r Tan	devised by the company	4
	Tarzanne – The Remix	Greg Cullen/Youth Community	40
	The Night Garden	Carys Evans	6
1996	Love Knot	-	3
	My Old Jumper	devised by the company	4
	Sky Blue Sea	Steve Burne	4
	The Secret Young Peoples Gathering	Stuart Blackburn	20
	Out of Mandragora/ Gadael Mandroga	devised by the company	3
	An Informers Duty	Greg Cullen/Youth Community	40
	Time of the Wolf	Gillian Clarke	4
	Maria's Baby	devised by the company	4
1997	The Constitution of the People	devised by the company	4
	Ladies Ladies	Louise Osborn	3
	Tall Stories	Greg Cullen/Youth Community	30
	Ablutions	devised by the company	5
	Andorra	trans Siwan Ellis	4
	Whispers in the Woods	Greg Cullen	50
1997	The Little Drummer Boy	Maureen Lawrence	6
1998	The Picture Writers	devised by the company	3
	Gwin Coch a Fodca	Wynford Ellis Owen	3
	Yr Uniad	devised by the company	3
	Silas Mariner	Greg Cullen	40
	The Shakespeare Project	devised by the company	1
	Morgiana's Dance	Maureen Lawrence	6

year	title	author	cast size
1999	The Apothecary's Story	devised by the company	4
	The Little Clay People/ Y Bobl Bach Clai	devised by the company	3
	Wind	Greg Cullen/Youth Community	50
	Safa'n Saff	Ian Staples	3
2000	Minimata	devised by the company	3
	Pillow of Glass	devised by the company	3
	Fi Fy Hun	devised by the company	3
	Cinderella	Charles Way	6
2001	Chance Children	Ian Yeoman	3

Sgript Cymru Company details on page 41

year	title	author	cast size
2000	Diwedd y Byd/Yr Hen Blant	Meic Povey	6
2001	Crazy Gary's Mobile Disco	Gary Owen	4
	Art and Guff	Catherine Tregenna	5
	Skipping for Toffee	Miriam Llywellyn	-
2002	Franco's Bastard	Dic Edwards	-

Sherman Theatre Company details on page 42

year	title	author	cast size
1991	A Kiss on the Bottom	Frank Vickery	5
	Y Llwybr Adref	Sian Edwards trans The Pathway Home	4
	Dracula	Sion Eirian	8
1992	Fern Hill	Mike Kenny	8
	Sleeping With Mickey Mouse	Frank Vickery	1
	Erogenous Zones	Frank Vickery	5
	Blodeuwedd	Sion Eirian	6
1994	A Generation Arises	Helen Griffin/Greg Cullen, Sion Eotian/Kelly Evans/Tim Rhys/ Linda Quinn/Charles Way/Roger Williams	4 + large cast
1995	Roots and Wings	Frank Vickery	6
	Surfing Carmarthen Bay	Roger Williams	3
	A Spell of Cold Weather	Charles Way	4
1996	Biting the Bullet	Frank Vickery	5
1997	Dangerous Women of the Mabinogion	Sharon Morgan/Gillian Clarke Angharad Devonald/Kate O'Reilly	large cast
	Break My Heart	Arnold Wesker	6
1998	Pullin the Wool	Frank Vickery	6
	Something Beginning With ...	Brendan Murray	4
1999	Secret Seven Save the World	Charles Way	7
	Everything Must Go	Patrick Jones	6
	Horrible Histories-Mad Millennium	Terry Deary	8
	Unprotected Sex	Patrick Jones	3
2000	Flesh and Blood	Helen Griffin	4
2001	Saturday Night Forever	Roger Williams	1
	From Cardiff with Love	devised	large cast

Slush Company details on page 44

year	title	author	cast size
2002	Fags	Gary Owen	4
	After Life	Gary Owen	-

Small World Theatre Company details on page 45

year	title	author	cast size
1991	Shades of Celtic Folk	devised	7
	In The Shadow of The City	Ann Shrosbree/Bill Hamblett music Adrian Wagner	2 + puppets
1992	Moving!	Ann Shrosbree/Bill Hamblett music Adrian Wagner	2 + puppets
	Padlock Jones	devised	2
	Manifiesto de la Selva	Ann Shrosbree/Bill Hamblett	2 + puppets
1995	Captain Slaughterboard Drops Anchor	Ann Shrosbree/Bill Hamblett trans Carol Burn Jones	3
1996	Manifiesto de la Selva 2	Carol Burn Jones	3
1997	File Not Found	Ann Shrosbree/Bill Hamblett	2
1998	Mufaro	Ann Shrosbree/Bill Hamblett	2
1999	Generation X	Act Your Age Intergenerational Theatre Group	18

Spectacle Theatre Company details on page 46

year	title	author	cast size
1991	Culture Change	devised by the company	2
1993	Delwedd	devised by the company	4
	Moon River - The Deal	Dic Edwards	4
	Cam Gwag	devised by the company	4
1994	My Name Is Me	devised by the company	2
1995	Sending Signals	Steve Davis	3
	Terfysg a Threfn	Matthew Arran	4
	Order and Disorder	Matthew Arran	4
1996	Without Words	devised by the company	4
1997	Kid	Dic Edwards	3
1998	POP	Steve Davis	3
	The Full Monty: homeless vid proj	Steve Davis	2+ community
1999	Through The Cat Flap	devised by the company	2
	Rhiwgarn Project - Underground	Steve Davis	2+ community
2000	Rhiwgarn Project - Balance	Steve Davis	2+ community
	Welsh Anthem RCT	Youth Theatre	community
	Over Milkwood	Dic Edwards	3
2001	Glyncornel - Youth Theatre	devised by the company	large cast

Steel Wasp Theatre Co Company details on page 47

year	title	author	cast size
1999	Garageland	Simon Harris	4
	Rising Tide	devised by the company/Kevin Matherick	5
2001	Moll Flanders	Clarre Luckam/George Stiles	5

Thin Language Company details on page 49

year	title	author	cast size
1993	Forever Yours Marie Lou	Michel Tremblay new version by Sian Evans	4
1995	Nothing To Pay	Caradoc Evans adpt Simon Harris	10
1997	Badfinger	Simon Harris	5

Touched Theatre Company details on page 51

year	title	author	cast size
1997	Sleep	Steve Marmion	3
1998	The Club	Steve Marmion	4

James Tyson

year	title	author	cast size
2000	Theorem / 02410351	James Tyson/Sara Rees	3
2001	The End of Theatre (or lovesongs for the 21st century/And the Night Illuminated the Night	James Tyson/Sara Rees	2

U-Man Zoo Company details on page 52

year	title	author	cast size
1994	Motorcity	devised by Richard Downing	10
1996	Vision 20 / 20	devised by Richard Downing	6
1997	The Dome	devised by Richard Downing	8
1998	Kite	devised by Richard Downing	12
1999	The Last Supper	devised by the company	9
2000	32 Wardrobes	devised by the company	12
2001	Water Banquet	devised by the company	6+
2000	Watertable	devised by the company	10+

Vanya Constant

year	title	author	cast size
1999	The Hydographer's Daughter	Vanya Constant	

Volcano Company details on page 53

year	title	author	cast size
1998	After the Orgy	-	2
1999	Moments of Madness	Paul Davies	5
2001	Torsk	-	3

Christine Watkins

year	title	author	cast size
1996	The Sea that Blazed	Made In Wales	4
1997	Black February/Mis Bach Du	WNO	Large community cast
1998	Queen of Hearts	Made In Wales	4

Welsh Fargo Stage Company Company details on page 55

year	title	author	cast size
1996	The Spirit of Enniskellen	Gordon Wilson adpt Michael Kelligan	1

WOT Theatre

year	title	author	cast size
1991	Cash	Mark Ryan	1
1997	Willows III-Waiting for Take Off	Mark Ryan	1
1998	Dr Jekyll & Mr Hyde	Mark Ryan	1

Cwmni Ballet Gwent Company details on page 12

year	title	choreographer	cast size
1991	Hiawatha	Darius James	-
1992	Cinderella Mossycoat	Darius James	-
1993	Beauty and the Beast	Darius James	-
1994	The Swan	Darius James	-
1995	Cinderella	Darius James	-
1996	Red Riding Hood and the Legend of Wolves	Darius James	-
1997	A Midsummer's Night Dream	Darius James	-
1998	The Tempest	Darius James	-
1999	Twelfth Night	Darius James	-
2000	As you Like it	Darius James	-
	Giselle Connotation	Darius James	-
2001	Romeo and Juliet	Darius James	-
2002	The Taming of the Shrew	Darius James	-

Carlson Dance Company Company details on page 15

year	title	choreographer	cast size
1992	Inner Corner	Emma & Sally Carlson	3
1993	Midnight Zone	Emma & Sally Carlson	3
1995	I.D.X	Emma & Sally Carlson	3
	Agonia	Emma & Sally Carlson	1
1996	6596	Emma & Sally Carlson	5
	Decay	Emma & Sally Carlson	1
1997	DK-Directions For Uso	Emma & Sally Carlson	3
1998	Frank	Emma & Sally Carlson	5
2000	Pantechnicon	Emma & Sally Carlson	2
	So Far Suite	Emma & Sally Carlson	2

Diversions Dance Company Company details on page 18

year	title	choreographer	cast size
1991	Icarus and Sons	Jem Treays	8
	Atlantique	Robert Kovich	8
	Never Enough	Dan Shapiro/Joanie Smith	8
	History of Collage Revisited	Bill T Jones	8
1992	Spirit catchers	Roy Campbell-Moore	8
	Vernacular Rhythms	Jerry Pearson	8
1993	Collecting Gravity	Terry Beck	8
	Exhibo	Kenneth Kvarnstrom	8
	Straight Jacket	Roy Campbell-Moore	8
1994	Dig	Terry Beck	8
	SVSPLKT	Daniel Ezralow	8

1995	Remembrance	Toni Mira	8
	Tableaux	Roy Campbell-Moore	8
1996	Strangers in the Night	Toni Mira	8
	Maxen's Dream	Beppie Blankert	8
1997	How Does it Feel	Roy Campbell-Moore	8
	From the Desert through the Forest	Matjaz Faric	8
1998	Lumen	Toni Mira	8
	Nowhere But Here	Bill T Jones	8
1999	Metropolis Roy	Roy Campbell-Moore	8
	Motets and Sawing	Orjan Anderson	8
2000	Constellation	Roy Campbell-Moore	8
	The Collector of Moments	Toni Mira	8
2001	Clearing	Zvi Gotheiner	8

Earthfall Company details on page 19

year	title	choreographer	cast size
1989	Earthfall	Jim Ennis/Jessica Cohen	5
1990	Nomads	Jim Ennis	4
	i and i #1	Jim Ennis/Jeffrey Burnett	2
1991	The Secret Soul of Things	Jim Ennis/Jessica Cohen	5
1992	The Intimate Jig	Jim Ennis/Jessica Cohen	6
1994	lives brief as photos	Jim Ennis/Jessica Cohen	6
1995	Girl Standing by the Lake	Jim Ennis/Jessica Cohen	5
	forever and ever	Jim Ennis/Jessica Cohen	5
1997/8	Fabulous Wounds	Jim Ennis/Jessica Cohen	8
1999/00	Rococo Blood	Jim Ennis/Jessica Cohen	6
2001	aD	Jim Ennis/Jessica Cohen	4

India Dance Wales Company details on page 30

year	title	choreographer	cast size
1993	Myths and Dance	Chitralekha Bolar, Kiran Ratna	3
1994	Shakuntala	Sunil Rajashekhar	14
1995	Navarasas	Mohan Kumar	3
1996	Mahabarata mabinogion	Kiran Ratna	5
1999	Ka;ighat Icons	Padmini Ramachandran	9
2000	Puranic Visions	Kiran Ratna	9
2001	The Tempest	Kiran Ratna	9

Sean Tuan John Company details on page 40

year	title	choreographer	cast size
-	Frederick's First Kiss	-	-
-	The Boy who Never Came Back	-	
-	Hanging Out With Jesus	-	-
-	Poor White Trash	-	-
-	Dances for Aliens	-	-
-	O Brutus	-	-

Marc Rees

year	title	choreographer	cast size
1995	Iddo Ef	Marc Rees	1
1999	Willows III - Waiting for Take off	Marc Rees	1
	Fist	Marc Rees	1
2000	Caligula Disco	Marc Rees	1

Jo Shapland (Man Troi) Company details on page 33

year	title	choreographer	cast size
1996	Chrysalis	Jo Shapland	3
1999	Zeitlupe	Jo Shapland	3-15
2000	Pedestal	Jo Shapland	1
2001	Soluna	Jo Shapland	1
	See the Wood through the Trees	Jo Shapland	

Simon Whitehead Company details on page 43

year	title	choreographer	cast size
1995/00	locator series	Simon Whitehead/Barnaby Oliver	10
1996	big muff	Simon Whitehead	
1996/97	salt / halen	Simon Whitehead	
1997	folcland	Simon Whitehead	
1998/99	tableland I, II,& III	Simon Whitehead	1, 2,
1999	skyclad	Simon Whitehead	
	Anemos	Simon Whitehead/Margaret Constantus	
2000	testing	Simon Whitehead	
	somasonicspirit	Simon Whitehead/Barnaby Oliver	3
	somasonics	Simon Whitehead/Barnaby Oliver	
	the rivers journey	Simon Whitehead/Rachel Rosenthal	
	stalks	Simon Whitehead/Barnaby Oliver	
2001	stalks (Cardiff)	Simon Whitehead	
	butterfly in the sun	Simon Whitehead	
	nightrider (ointment)	Simon Whitehead	
	wooden horse	Simon Whitehead	
	haunts	Simon Whitehead	
	vein (Quebec)	Simon Whitehead	

SELECTED BIBLIOGRAPHY
LLYFRYDDIAETH

Theatre in Wales/Y Theatr yng Nghymru:

Stage Welsh
David Adams (Gomer 1996)

Staging Wales
ed. Anna-Marie Taylor (University of Wales Press 1997)

State of Play
ed.Hazel Walford Davies (Gomer 1998)

Marketing/Marchnata:

A Guide to Audience Development
Heather Maitland (Arts Council of England 1997)

The Golden Guide: Marketing for Touring
Heather Maitland (Arts Council of England 1998)

The Silver Guide: Marketing for Touring Companies with Limited Resources
(Arts Council of England 1997)

The Marketing Manual
Heather Maitland (Arts Marketing Association 2001)

Fundraising/Codi Arian:

The Arts Funding Guide
ed. Susan Forrester, David Lloyd (Directory of Social Change 2002)

The Complete Fundraising Handbook
ed. Nina Botting, Michael Norton (Directory of Social Change and ICFM 2001)

A Guide to European Union Funding for the Voluntary Sector
Peter Sluiter, Laurence Wattier (Directory of Social Change 1999)

Your Way Through the Labyrinth: a guide to European funding for NGO's
(ECAS 2002)

The Youth Funding Guide
Nicola Eastwood (Directory of Social Change 2002)

Management/Rheolaeth:

Just About Managing
Sandy Adirondack (London Voluntary Service Council 1998)

Managing Without Profit: the art of managing third sector organisations
Mike Hudson (Penguin 1999)

Reference/Cyfeirlyfrau:

Arts Networking in Europe
ed. Rod Fisher (Arts Council of England 1997)

British Performing Arts Yearbook
ed. Louise Head (Rhinegold Publishing Limited 2001)

Performing Arts Yearbook for Europe
ed. Karin Junker (Arts Publishing International Limited 2001)

Selected Anthologies/Antholegau Dethol:

Act One Wales: Thirteen One Act Plays
ed. Phil Clark (Seren 1997)

Greg Cullen: Three Plays
ed. Brian Mitchell (Seren 1998)

Dic Edwards: Three Plays
(Oberon 1992)

Dic Edwards: Three Plays
ed. Brian Michell (Seren 1998)

Lucy Gough: Three Plays
ed. Brian Michell (Seren 2000)

Act One Wales: Thirteen One Act Plays
ed. Phil Clark (Seren 1997)

Edward Thomas: Three Plays
ed. Brian Mitchell (Seren 1994)

Charles Way: Three Plays
ed. Brian Mitchell (Seren 1994)